W9-DHI-673

The Next Generation

SUNY Series in American Jewish Society in the 1990s
Barry A. Kosmin and Sidney Goldstein, editors

THE NEXT GENERATION

Jewish Children and Adolescents

Ariela Keysar, Barry A. Kosmin,
and Jeffrey Scheckner

State University of New York Press

Cover photograph courtesy
of Rocky Raco

Published by
State University of New York Press, Albany

©2000 State University of New York

For information, address State University of New York Press
State University Plaza, Albany, New York 12246

Production by Dana Foote
Marketing by Dana E. Yanulavich

Library of Congress Cataloging-in-Publication Data

Keysar, Ariela, 1955–
The next generation : Jewish children and adolescents / Ariela Keysar, Barry A.
Kosmin, and Jeffrey Scheckner.
p. cm. — (SUNY series in American Jewish society in the 1990s)
Includes bibliographical references and index.
ISBN 0–7914-4543-7 (alk. paper) — ISBN 0–7914–4544–5 (pbk. : alk. paper)
1. Jewish children—United States—Social conditions—20th century—Statistics.
2. Jewish teenagers—United States—Social conditions—20th century—Statistics.
3. Jews—Socialization—United States—Statistics.   4. 1990 National Jewish Population
Survey.   I. Kosmin, Barry A. (Barry Alexander)   II. Scheckner, Jeffrey, 1953–   III. Title.
IV. Series.
E184.36.S65 K49 2000
305.23—dc21   00-024953

10 9 8 7 6 5 4 3 2 1

For our children:
Ethan
Peta-Doris, Guy, and Jessica
Joshua and Harlan

CONTENTS

LIST OF TABLES AND FIGURES

Tables

Figures

FOREWORD

The Next Generation: Jewish Children and Adolescents is the fifth monograph to be published in the series, *American Jewish Society in the 1990s*, based on the landmark 1990 National Jewish Population Survey. The NJPS was envisioned in 1986 by the National Technical Advisory Committee on Jewish Population Studies (NTAC) of the Council of Jewish Federations, and sponsored by CJF. The editors of this series of monographs are NTAC Chair Dr. Sidney Goldstein, G. H. Crooker University Professor Emeritus and Professor Emeritus of Sociology at Brown University, and Dr. Barry Kosmin, co-author of the present monograph, who in 1990 was the Director of the North American Jewish Data Bank at the City University of New York, Graduate Center. The first monograph in the series was *Jews on the Move*, by Sidney Goldstein and Alice Goldstein (1996). It was followed by *Gender Equality and American Jews* by Moshe Hartman and Harriet Hartman (1996); *Jewish Choices: American Jewish Denominationalism* by Bernard Lazerwitz, J. Alan Winter, Arnold Dashefsky, and Ephraim Tabory (1998); and *Jewish Life and American Culture* by Sylvia Barack Fishman (2000).

With its focus on children and adolescents, this monograph looks ahead toward American Judaism in the twenty-first century. In 1990, the subjects of this study ranged from newborns to 17-year-olds. From among them will spring the leaders of the Jewish community in America in decades to come. Moreover, by studying children and adolescents, this monograph sheds light on the most important institution in Jewish life, the family. It explores the evolving composition of Jewish families, including single parenthood and intermarriage; analyzes the impact of different family structures on the well-being and religious upbringing of children; and examines the role of parents in ensuring Jewish continuity.

United Jewish Communities, a partnership of United Jewish Appeal and the Council of Jewish Federations, is sponsoring another National Jewish Population Survey in 2000, which will be even larger than the 1990 study. Research based on the 2000 survey will be published over the coming decade. The 1990 survey, while it will no longer be the most current, will remain a vital resource, both as a baseline for comparison and as a treasury of data about the American Jewish community at a turning point in its history.

Barry A. Kosmin
Director
Institute for Jewish Policy
Research
London, UK

Sidney Goldstein
Population Studies and
Training Center
Brown University
Providence, RI

ACKNOWLEDGMENTS

The authors of this volume wish to thank Sidney Goldstein, coeditor of the monograph series, for his generous guidance and constructive criticism. We appreciate the support of our "buddies" who provided helpful advice and ideas in a peer review system: Rela M. Geffen, Vivian Klaff, and Egon Mayer. Deborah Bursztyn ably programmed and created maps and charts. The authors benefited from the statistical advice of David Rindskopf. Aaron Beim, Peter Coy, Larry Grossman, and Jay Mandel made valuable editing suggestions. Rakefet Strauss and Lucy Steinitz provided research assistance. Jim Schwartz's support enabled us to complete this project. Finally, we are grateful to the dedicated secretaries of CJF, Selma Devins, Don Hulbert, Florence Koppelman, and those of the Center for Jewish Studies at CUNY, Luann Dragone and Robin Reevie.

INTRODUCTION AND PLAN FOR ANALYSIS

This monograph on American Jewish children and their socialization into a minority subculture in an open society has been written for a varied audience: academics, educators, youth leaders, social workers, and anyone interested in the study of children of a minority religious group. Different types of readers will find different chapters of interest. Topics covered include demography, household structure, social welfare, affiliation, denomination, parental fertility, Jewish education, geographic differences, communal participation, religious socialization, interfaith status of the household, and population projections. These diverse topics and the nature of our data sources lend themselves to different treatments. Some sections of the monograph are descriptive (chapter 2), some are analytical (chapter 5), some are more theoretical (chapter 4), while others use complicated statistical models (chapters 4 and 7). Readers will be guided accordingly. We hope that they will find their appropriate topic and analysis at a suitable level of complexity.

PLAN FOR ANALYSIS

A primary goal in this monograph is to examine which theories of socialization (chapter 1) are applicable to young American Jews, those under the age of 18. To this end, we extract data on the microlevel (individuals or households) as well as on the macrolevel (children and adolescents collectively). We investigate whether the socialization process that takes place in the family also needs assistance by institutional and community intervention. Some of the specific questions addressed are the following:

- What is the overall demography of the Jewish child population in the United States?
- How do the household composition and the economic and social status of a family affect the religious upbringing of the children?
- How does the religious identity of the parents affect how children are raised?
- What are the consequences of intermarriage vs. Jewish marriage on Jewish children's lives? What is the impact on the next generation?
- How do factors such as neighborhood, density of the Jewish population, and the level of Jewish environment outside the home affect the Jewish socialization of the child?
- What role does Jewish communal intervention—Jewish community centers, Jewish camps, Jewish youth groups, Jewish day care—play in Jewish socialization?
- Will the number of Jewish children increase, decrease, or remain the same over the next twenty years?

A major thrust of this volume is to show how different types of environments and household structures affect the long-term process of Jewish socialization. The basis thesis is that greater the exposure to a Jewish environment, both in and outside the home, the more likely the child will participate in Jewish community activities as an adult. In Chapter 6 we look at the impact of communal intervention in the Jewish socialization process. Chapter 7 attempts to project the future size and composition of the Jewish child population using several demographic assumptions. These concluding chapters display the potential for future Jewish vitality among the child population.

Pluralism and diversity are ongoing themes. The conflicts and challenges to the individual child and the family living in a free society need to be recognized. We make no attempt to examine mental health, social psychology, emotional stability, or deviant behavior. Further, we do not review the impact that broader environmental factors have on the individual child. The questions asked in our primary data source, the National Jewish Population Survey of 1990 (NJPS), did not provide the information needed for such evaluations. Similarly, we do not attempt to assess whether being Jewish and having a Jewish upbringing is "good" or "bad" for the social and psychological well-being of children. Although we provide models that incorporate attention to increased Jewish involvement, we also avoid suggesting whether one form of Jewish expression or association is better, or of greater value, than another.

CHAPTER 1

THEORY AND METHODOLOGY

RELIGIOUS SOCIALIZATION

Jewish continuity is at risk in the contemporary United States. The future of American Jewry is jeopardized by the erosion of the cultural integrity of the group and the blurring of its boundaries in an open society. For the purpose of our discussion, Jewish continuity is defined as the retention and enhancement of the quality of Jewish life. This is accomplished by the teaching of Judaism, its values and beliefs, as well as concern for the unity and continuation of the Jewish people. The problem of maintaining continuity is not unique to Jews; it challenges all minority groups that confront the problem of raising their young people in a unique heritage within a diverse larger society. Most minority communities want their children to maintain their identity over time while fully participating as Americans and enjoying the benefits and the opportunities this country offers. Being at home in two societies and cultures is a difficult challenge that creates multiple tensions—within the larger society, the subculture, the family, the individual, and particularly across the generations.

In the 1930s, in a less pluralistic America, Stonequist developed the concept of the "marginal man." He suggested that these "dilemmas are most difficult to resolve in the case of the Jews . . . the marginal Jew oscillates forward and backward, out of his group and then back into his group. . . . The marginal Jew tends to remain persistently in the psychological center of the cultural conflict" (Stonequist 1937, 133). The portrait of the marginal Jew was very much bound up with the issue of immigration and the clash between the first and second generations. In the 1990s Jews are primarily third and fourth generation Americans. Moreover, the social environment for Jews is more welcoming, and individual Jews are no longer marginal in American society. In fact, contemporary Jews are largely acculturated and assimilated Americans. Thus, from the community perspective the main concern is now boundary maintenance in the pursuit of group survival. In the light of these new circumstances, our research approach in this volume, which is structural and ecological rather than psychological, is perhaps more relevant to the challenges facing American Jewry at this time.

In the American Jewish context one has to be aware of the distinction between Jewish identity and Jewish identification. According to Himmelfarb (1982, 31), "Jewish identity is one's sense of self with regard to being Jewish," whereas "Jewish identification is the process of thinking and acting in a manner that indicates involvement with and attachment to Jewish life." Liebman (1973) shows that the early studies of Jewish identity were concerned with integration, whereas later studies, stressing group survival, have focused on Jewish identification. Our assessment focuses essentially on the Jewish identification of the younger generation since cultural continuity is maintained by the transmission of values from one generation to the next.

The continuity of any religious or cultural group depends on the socialization of its members and their children. Individuals learn religious values, attitudes, and sentiments which become part of their own personality patterns. Socialization begins in infancy and ends only at death. Throughout this process the group exerts an influence upon the personalities of the individual members. As people acquire their identities, they accept, reject, or remain neutral to religious ideals. Religious value systems attempt to channel personal responses to religious ends. Yet, these responses must be learned and internalized. Generally, religious socialization attempts to develop a basic sense of discipline so that one learns to postpone, modify, or even forego gratification in order to reach some religiously sanctioned future goal. This is particularly true of Judaism, which more than other religions tends to emphasize behavior and ritual (mitzvot) rather than faith.

The role of religion is of greater importance to those who have the responsibility of raising the younger generation. "Most modern parents claim that they look to religion as an ally in instilling morals and values in a society . . . many are concerned that they do not have control over their children's lives, and they seek a community that supports them in protecting children from society's evils, such as drugs, gangs, teen-age pregnancies, and the loss of academic motivation" (Kosmin and Lachman 1993, 237). However, religious socialization goes beyond behavior to encompass the teaching of religious roles and their supporting values. As people continue their involvement in religious institutions, they learn specific skills of particular value to their religious group, such as language, prayers, and music. Strong institutional socialization leads to membership conformity; socialization brings assimilation to the specific religious culture. A complicating factor for American Jews compared to other religious groups in the United States is the ethnic component of their identity. This means that some Jews self-identify as nonreligious or secular Jews. The transmission of secular Jewish culture is a difficult task for parents and for social scientists. It is also difficult to measure on a separate scale from religious socialization. Rather than exclude this population, we have chosen to follow historical precedent and include it in the overall Jewish population.

SOCIALIZATION OF CHILDREN

Social science literature asserts that parents are the primary agents for transferring cultural and religious elements across generations. Much of the earliest stages of the process is conceptualized in both psychology and sociology as a child's *socialization:* the process whereby individuals acquire the skills, motives, standards, and behavioral style that will enable them to conform to the expectations of their present and future social environment (Hetherington and Morris 1978).

Children's lives are shaped by encounters with others who define a socially organized world. Socialization is also defined as "the process by which we learn the ways of a given society or social group so that we can function within it" (Elkin and Handel 1984, 4). The learning process is not limited to specific kinds of knowledge or modes of learning: some, such as the use of language, are overt and observable, and others are covert. The resulting behaviors are guided through a process of social learning for membership in the cultural group, which is characterized by their language, foods, rituals, folklore, and patterns of child rearing (Elkin and Handel 1984, 14).

The primary agent in the child's socialization process is the immediate family. Although the family is not the sole socialization agent, it has special importance in immediately placing the newborn child in a certain social position in terms of class, status, culture, and geographic area. The child's peer group and school also have important functions. All these elements prescribe specific values that are transmitted to the child, and even affect the type of interactions the child will have with others.

In American society of the 1990s, there is a political and philosophical debate over moral questions that focus on education and family values. Children today live in a global society with unfettered mass communication. They are exposed from their earliest years to a greater number and a wider assortment of messages from powerful mass media than any previous generation. This study, and previous studies in the monograph series, show the difficulties of preserving a minority culture in this situation. Whether we categorize the contemporary American society, in which the present generation of Jewish children are raised, as secular, or Christian, or even a mixture of the two, it certainly provides neither a Jewish ambience nor a Jewish environment. This makes socializing Jewish children far more challenging and complex.

Children perceive the other people they are in contact with as role models for behavior. For minority group members, will the reference group come from the majority or the minority culture? For example, a Jewish child who sees his or her parents going to the synagogue every Sabbath may be more inclined to go to synagogue later in life. By their behavior, adults define for the children how to respond to the social reality. Peers also can reinforce prosocial behavior (Strain et al. 1976). Socialization takes place in numerous settings—at home, in the playground, in youth groups, in camps, at school, or in the synagogue. These settings can represent either the majority or the minority culture.

Central to the normal cognitive and emotional growth of children is the development of self-identity through processes of social cognition: differentiation of the self from others, of one set of humans from another by gradations of closeness and salience to one's own being (Flavell 1985). The historical development of the Jewish population requires the distinction between public identity, which is a person's traits as they appear to others, and self-identity, which is the person's private version of his or her pattern of traits (Miller 1963). For Jewish children growing up in a Christian society, this distinction may evoke conflicts on an individual level, in a family setting, and in the larger society—in the neighborhood or at school.

Beyond the formation of the self is the formation of roles. Like identity and the self, roles are not fixed but change throughout the individual's life. Moreover, one always has multiple roles at any point in time. The individual is not a passive actor in socialization; the relationship between the individual and the socialization process is dynamic, and individuals can modify the outcomes of their socialization. The individual's identity arises from the social context, or more specifically, the social categories into which the child is socialized. The child can be socialized simultaneously to different social categories—the ethnic group to which he or she belongs, the national identity, and the religious group. These categories form the individual's various identities—as a citizen, as part of a specific religion or ethnic culture, gender, social class, etc.

The identity of the individual child is a complex web of cognitions, conceptions, emotions, motives, values, and role repertoires stored as symbolic knowledge that can be accessed on cue. Yet many of the factors that contribute to the development of this complex web and its basic organization are still but partly understood (Harter 1983). Family, neighborhood, and school provide children a chance for contact and experimental identification with other children and adults of all ages. A child begins early to build a hierarchy of expectations of what it will feel like to be older. These expectations become part of an identity and are verified, step by step, later in life (Erikson 1968).

The process of socialization itself entails specialized learning components, such as psycho-emotional identification with significant others (e.g., parents and siblings), acquisition of norms, roles and values, and the adaptation of the self to social boundary definition (Perry and Perry 1983). Jewish society has its own culture, its body of "knowledge, belief, art, morals, law, custom, and any other capabilities and habits acquired by man as a member of society" (Tylor 1958). As Jewish children learn the culture of their society, they become socialized beings. A norm is an "implicit rule defining the appropriate pattern of behavior in a recurring situation" (Elkin and Handel 1984, 10). While Jewish values, like other values, are more general than norms, they are not behavior directed, but general concepts that serve as social criteria for distinguishing between "right" and "wrong."

In different societies, children experience different socialization processes, thereby developing a variety of personal traits for participation in society. This process influences parents and other child-rearing agents to use particular techniques in raising their children. "Child-rearing is culturally organized formulae which generally enable parents to successfully teach their children those language, cognitive, motivational and social competencies, i.e. the nature of the personal attributes, required to function competently in their culture" (Ogbu 1979, 10).

Children from any culture learn social roles and the statuses that are attached to these roles, i.e., their position in the social structure, and the obligations and rights that are related to specific statuses. All children also learn to identify themselves and others by social class and cultural group, which according to Max Weber, are associated with specific values and a way of life.

In our complex contemporary society, multiple socialization agencies, particularly extrafamilial institutions such as the media and advertising, play roles in forming children's religious outlooks. Consequently today's parents have less of a monopoly and control on their children's worldview.

ADOLESCENT DEVELOPMENT

'olescent years are a time of significant physical, emotional, and cognitive
  \ crucial aspect in the transition to adolescence is the transformed relation-

ship between parent and child, who must renegotiate the sense of control, responsibility, and autonomy. This is a transitional period in which adolescents gradually convert childhood roles and orientations to those characterizing adulthood (Erikson 1977). Adolescents encounter new demands as the childhood milieu, namely parents and family, is replaced by "society" (Erikson 1968). The transitional period, which is complicated in all societies, is especially difficult for young people who are members of a minority group considering the diverse and complex roles they need to assume. Adolescents in such societies have to learn to perform a variety of roles that often clash with one another, primarily with those roles associated with the majority group.

In the search for self-definition, the adolescent interacts with his or her environment and seeks out those to whom to relate. The peer group, rather than the family, increasingly dominates the adolescent's thinking and behavior, and begins to serve as a catalyst for identity development. The peer group is another socialization agent whose influence grows stronger as the child advances in age. "In the American society the child's own contemporaries have great importance. The child learns to give great weight to what other children think of his behavior, to want to gain their approval and avoid their disapproval. In societies in which the peer group is an important socializing agent, there may be greater conformity to age group standards. Undoubtedly the use of peer group as a socializing agent by Americans produces a different sense of self, a person who always pays attention to what others are doing in order to get a signal for what he himself should do" (Martin and Stendler 1959, 195–196).

Young people acquire different personal resources from different socialization agencies. Psychological development, mainly identity formation, is attributed to the intimate family context, while the instrumental-based school contributes to the development of general cognitive skills and information. The informal peer group and youth association are more effective in developing interpersonal skills and fostering universal norms and moral orientations (Rapoport 1989). Following Rapoport's overview, these resources can be translated into the Jewish realm. Simply, the home environment is responsible in passing the tradition and building Jewish identity, whereas Jewish schools teach religious skills, Jewish history, and culture, and Jewish youth groups and the summer camps embedded in them provide Jewish role models and peers, thus accommodating further Jewish social contacts.

An influential aspect of the peer group is the socio-economic, ethnic, and religious background of its members. While there is a tendency for adolescents, like people of all ages, to share the most with those of similar backgrounds, the ethnic or religious character of a peer group can either solidify or weaken the individual's attachment to it. While it is natural to move away from parental domination, the adolescent may also resent the parents' culture and religious beliefs. For example, a youth from a particular religious group may intentionally associate with a peer group composed of individuals who are not from his or her religious background. When this occurs, the pressure to assimilate to the standards of the new group may be accentuated.

Yet in some ways, for the current generation of American Jews, peer pressure poses less of a problem than in the past. We do not now find the conflict between immigrant parents and American children, since over 90 percent of Jews are U.S. born and therefore there is no "new society" to stimulate the young to rebel (Eisenstadt 1956). Furthermore, Eisenstadt claims that the greater the "familism" the smaller the "adolescent problem." For such reasons and on the basis of contemporary evidence, Perry London asserts that "Jewish kids in the United States are . . . for the most part, not much involved with drug addiction, delinquency, crime, and dropping out of school. They are among the highest achieving groups in the United States in school grades, scholarships and college attendance. They are well socialized to American middle class society's ideals" (London 1990, 7). The pattern of college enrollment and SAT scores supports this claim (Kosmin and Lachman 1992).

How likely are adolescents to adopt a value system somewhat similar to that of their parents? As discussed earlier, adolescence is a period of searching for a separate and personal identity, the time for emancipation—to become emotionally independent from parents and other adults. Emancipation theory explains the generational gap by asserting that adolescents reject their parents' religious values and become less traditional. In contrast, social learning theory holds that religious values are transmitted by the modeling and internalization of moral standards, such that adolescents' values tend to resemble those of their parents (Dudley and Dudley 1986).

Parents typically teach their children religious beliefs and further shape their beliefs and practices through the selection of a denomination and the intensity of their religious commitment (see Ozorak 1989). During the course of adolescence, when young people question, reason, and have greater social opportunities to exchange ideas and compare their beliefs to others', changes in religious outlook and behavior often occur. Research has recognized the important role parents play in transmitting religious beliefs to their children into adolescence (Parker and Gaier 1980). There is less evidence that peers influence adolescents' religiousness, although members of church youth groups seem susceptible to peer pressure (Hoge and Petrillo 1978). Ozorak (1989) attempted to weigh the relative impact of parents' religiousness, closeness to peers and parents, and affiliation on religious commitment and change among adolescents. She reported that parents' religious affiliation and practices were positively related to religiousness among early and middle adolescents. Family closeness was also negatively associated with modification of religious practices, she found, concluding that "parents' affiliation and their faith in that affiliation act as cognitive anchors from which children's beliefs evolve over time" (Ozorak 1989, 460).

Hoge et al. (1982) compared the effect of parental values on children's values with the effect of membership in the Catholic, Baptist, and Methodist churches. They found that denominational membership had a slightly stronger effect, concluding that young people are influenced by the larger social structure because over time they obtain their values from extrafamilial culture as much as from their parents.

Joseph Erickson developed a model in which familial influence was hypothesized to act indirectly through the adolescent's religious education. Looking at the three critical social influences in young people's religious developments—parents, peers, and religious education—he argued that adolescent religious development is triggered by home religious habits and education. Following Cornwall's (1988) concept of "channeling," that is, the indirect social influence parents have over their children, Erickson argues that "parents direct their children to other social influences, and it is these influences which are more salient. Of particular interest is the strength of the religious education variable" (Erickson 1992, 149).

Thus, the adolescent's attitude toward his or her ethnic or religious background in relation to the peer group is fashioned by a number of factors, including "his sense of personal security, the warmth and constructiveness of the family constellation in infancy and childhood, the attitudes prevailing in the immediate neighborhood and how they are fostered in the schools and religious institutions . . . and the strength and nature of the individual's feelings of belonging to his minority group" (Rothman 1965, 12). Theoretically, the more traditional the home environment, the more likely the adolescent will associate with peers of similar background or join a youth group with the same type of individuals.

The formation of a specifically Jewish identity has its roots in the home and the tradition of the individual, and depends on whether the parents provide a clear and positive feeling of belonging to Judaism, and whether that feeling is carried through in peer group interaction and enhanced through a support system like a Jewish youth group. "Peer groups are frequently used as a vehicle for training pro-social behaviors. Not only is group training more convenient but the dynamics of the interaction between members of the group may also provide particular opportunities for learning that cannot be derived from dyadic interaction. Thus peers serve as stimulators" (Rubin and Ross 1982, 157).

Jewish youth groups and summer camps are among the informal socialization agencies that can facilitate the passage to adulthood by providing multiple opportunities for trial and error behavior (Rapoport and Kahane 1988). This exploratory behavior, which enables adolescents to experiment with a variety of rules and roles, is essential for youth development (Coleman 1974). In addition, these informal socialization agencies within a peer context allow adolescents to experience the transitional passage to adulthood on their own terms with little adult supervision (Kahane 1975; Rapoport and Kahane 1988). In the Jewish context, members of Jewish youth groups and participants in summer camps learn to select, reformulate, and integrate concepts of social reality and thereby shape their own Jewish identity.

Informal socialization agencies have the potential to create the transition in terms of role development. These type of agencies are likely to provide a context in which the transition period to adulthood is institutionalized, the role repertoire is expanded, whereby child-oriented roles are replaced by adult-oriented ones (Rapoport and Kahane 1988). Jewish youth groups and summer camps are valuable because they enable young people to meet positive Jewish role models, particularly their counselors. These staff serve as accessible young Jewish models who are relatively close to the teenagers in age and who chose to adopt a positive Jewish identity. Furthermore, summer camps and in particular the Israel Experience, a teenage educational summer program in Israel (Chazan 1997), are intense group experiences in which Jewish teens spend several weeks together as part of a tightly knit group of like-minded peers. They eat, sleep, engage in sports, and socialize with this group and develop intense loyalty to the other teens and to the Jewish group as a whole. Long-term connection between different forms of formal and informal Jewish education and increased adult Jewish identity and involvement are suggested in several Jewish studies (Cohen 1995; Mittelberg 1994; Phillips 1997). If the community is interested in maximizing the possibilities of increased Jewishness of its youngsters as they become adults, such experiences are a worthwhile investment.

Moreover, reinforcing young people's Jewish identity is especially advantageous during adolescence since adolescents are gifted with the ability to adjust to new ideas and ideals. This is the time to expose them to new role models so they can accept a more explicitly Jewish outlook.

SOCIALIZATION INTO A SUBCULTURE

George Mead argued that the self is fully developed only when the person is socialized to his or her social group and its institutional manifestations (Mead 1934, 155). Just as the individual depends on the social group for development, the group relies on the socialization of the individual roles in the community. "The complex cooperative process and activities and institutional functioning of organized human society are also possible only insofar as every individual involved in them . . . can take the general attitudes of all other such individuals with reference to these processes and activities and institutional functioning . . . and can direct his own behavior accordingly" (Mead 1934, 155). If individuals are not socialized according to community norms and values, the community will eventually experience disorganization and finally disintegrate. Thus, the continued existence of the social community depends on the effective socialization of its members.

Modern societies generally include many subcultures, each with a unique way of life, but all part of the same society and sharing important common elements. As we have shown above, the concept of culture is central to socialization. The relationship between the subculture and the larger society is complex and the lines between a specific subculture and the larger society are not always clearly drawn. This complex relationship raises important questions: How do those involved in the subculture participate in the larger society? How is the community defined and where are its borders? What are the distinguishing elements of the subculture, and how are they transmitted to new members? Is the subculture undergoing assimilation?

In some cases, such as that of Orthodox Jews, the boundaries are distinctly defined and observable. Kallen, who studied Orthodox Jews in Toronto, found that "traditional Judaic prescriptions and proscriptions provided strong boundary-maintaining mechanisms ensuring that social relationships with outsiders were confined to the public sphere . . . primary relationships were confined to fellow Jews, and private Jewish institutions remained largely insulated from the cultural influences of Anglo-Canadian society" (Kallen 1977, 66).

Transmission of cultural practices occurs at different stages of the socialization process. Children come to understand their ethnic or cultural group first in terms of external manifestation such as customs, choice of clothing, holiday celebrations, food, neighborhood, and rituals; as they grow older they internalize the substantive aspect of their culture, such as the belief system and the norms and values that are related to it.

Another important stage in socialization to a subculture is when the child learns to distinguish between members of his or her cultural group and others. This marks an important step in the development of cultural identification with one's group, and the sense of borders between "us" and "them." At this stage, the child feels that he or she belongs to a certain collectivity, and internalizes the collective identity. The process of internalizing collective identity can be reinforced by participation in activities that are unique to the subculture, such as holiday celebrations, learning a special language, participating in ceremonies, and learning values, legends, stories, etc. The child develops what Gordon Allport named "ego extension," the identification of the collective as "mine." An example of this is the interest of American Jews in Israel (Elkin and Handel 1984, 102).

Elkin and Handel also point to three important aspects of subculture. First, the individual's status in the society is partly determined by his or her subculture. Second, the child's earliest role models are usually members of the social group to which the child belongs. Third, the child's significant others, the primary socialization agents, are mostly adherents of the same subculture, and therefore the development of the child's self is based in this subculture. For example, the religious identity of a Jewish child is derived from the group. From the child's point of view, being a Jew is a religious and cultural identity; from society's point of view, the individual's identity also implies a specific social position and a set of statuses that are related to this position.

The most important agent of cultural identity socialization is the family. "Unless children learn and experience their basic ethnic identity within the family or other primary groups, it is unlikely that they will ever strongly feel it thereafter" (Elkin and Handel 1984, 110). This has crucial implications for social policy, especially for families that are not religiously endogamous.

Among Roman Catholic families, a marked gap between traditional and modern expectations of family responsibility was identified several decades ago (Thomas 1951). The decline of home religious training was seen as posing a threat to the continuity of traditional religious ideals. The solution suggested, if the religious group was not to lose its younger members, was a revitalized program of religious education through parochial schools. This policy shifted the onus for intergenerational religious and cultural transmission from the family to a formal institution. Faced by similar challenges and with the acknowledgment that schooling is an important agent of religious socialization, the Jewish community's response has been to replicate the Catholic model by revitalizing and intensifying religious education through greater investment by the community and parents. This is reflected in the 1990 NJPS, which showed that the proportion of children receiving a Jewish day-school education had risen considerably.

The general trend today is a division of labor between socialization agencies and gradually for institutions to take over from the family more of the responsibility for socialization of children and adolescents. This research will demonstrate that the American Jewish family is not immune from the stresses that have undermined the traditional nuclear family, and as a result, the Jewish family today has less capacity for socializing children and preserving the minority Jewish subculture without external assistance from communal institutions.

The insights from socialization theory, when applied to the specific needs of Jewish continuity in the contemporary United States, suggest that the Jewish community faces a complex crisis on a number of levels: the individual, the household and family, and the local and national communities. Before providing an overview of the current social and cultural environment of American Jewish children, we describe the data that provide insights into the Jewish population whose characteristics, behaviors, and attitudes we will be examining.

THE 1990 NJPS SURVEY METHODOLOGY

The decennial national census has never collected data on the American Jewish population either as an ethnic or religious group. This infrastructural void has disadvantaged the institutions of American Jewry in planning for their constituency. In 1970 and 1990 the federation system commissioned national sample surveys to resolve this problem.

The overall research design for the 1990 National Jewish Population Survey incorporated a pretest as well as a multistage survey over a period of fifteen months, which included an initial screening phase lasting sixty-two weeks, a recontact phase, and a final in-depth survey of 2,500 households. In April 1989, the Council of Jewish Federations, a national organization of the Jewish voluntary sector, commissioned the ICR Survey Research Group of Media, Pennsylvania, to begin collecting data in a multistage telephone survey utilizing their twice-weekly national omnibus survey, EXCEL. The data were collected only for the civilian noninstitutional population in telephone households.

The first stage, designed to identify a potential sample of Jewish households, involved sampling over 125,000 households using the GENESYS random digit dialing (RDD) system. One thousand households were contracted in each of 125 successive rounds over the period from April 1989 to July 1990. An adult respondent was chosen in each household, using the last birthday method of selection. The procedure allowed for equal probability of Jewish and non-Jewish households to be selected from every state in the continental United States. Representation of Alaska and Hawaii was incorporated into the national sample in the third stage of the survey. In all, among the 125,000 households screened, 5,139 households containing one or more "qualified" Jews were identified by the first screening phase. Individuals could qualify on the basis of any of these four criteria: religion, "considering" themselves Jewish, raised Jewish, or having a Jewish parent. (See Appendix, p. 109, for the screening questions and more details about criteria for qualification.) Only 2.3 percent of the respondents refused to reply to the question regarding religion.

Beginning in June 1989, qualified Jewish households were recontacted. The goal of this phase was to minimize losses due to attrition of the sample between the initial screening and the in-depth Jewish survey planned for the spring and early summer of 1990 and to ascertain the qualification of each member in the household, since the in-depth survey required a randomly selected adult Jewish respondent.

The National Jewish Population Survey (NJPS) database consists primarily of the in-depth household survey conducted in the third stage. Of the previously screened households, qualified households were interviewed during May–July 1990, using an extensive questionnaire, which included socio-demographic and economic questions alongside a wide array of attitudinal and behavioral characteristics related to the Jewish identity and practice of all household members.

DEFINITIONS AND QUALIFYING POINTS

For purposes of this monograph, we have defined the child population as those individuals aged 0–17. Several questions in the NJPS survey instrument requested information on the age of household members and their relationship to the respondent. By focusing on households with children under 18, we are able to undertake a descriptive analysis of these households and to assess the behaviors of the children present.

The *Core Jewish* child population referred to consistently throughout this monograph belongs to three subgroups: (1) *Born Jews* whose religion is Judaism (BJR); (2) converts, known as *Jews by Choice* (JBC); (3) and secular Jews, or *Jews with No Religion* (JNR). While all three groups are considered Core Jews, only the first two are counted as *Jews by Religion* (JBR). The non-Core child population is referred to as *Jewish Children of Other Religions* (JCOR). These are children with some Jewish background in terms of descent or ethnicity, but who were not considered Jewish at the time of the survey. In an attempt to report on all the children identified in NJPS, we begin our descriptive analysis in chapter 2 with a quantification of these different types, and provide some basic characteristics, such as population numbers and geographic distribution. It is important to begin with an inclusive analysis of the total NJPS child population. Although not part of the Core, JCOR children may be considered part of the Jewish population in a broader sense; they may be exposed to some degree of Jewish practice in their homes which could lead to a sense of Jewish identity later in life. However, the primary concentration in this volume is on the Core Jewish population, as it is this group on which the theme, socialization of the Jewish child, is based. It is also the Core Jewish population that is the primary focus and concern of most Jewish communal organizations' attempts to encourage Jewish practice and Jewish continuity.

There were 1,489 cases of children (Core and non-Core) among the total NJPS enumerated population, and this universe is used for particular discussions. Of these cases of children, 927 qualified as Core and 562 as non-Core.

NJPS provided data on individual household members and on household characteristics. Some variables that we analyze—such as gender, age, and education—refer to characteristics of individual household members. Other variables relate to the household unit, such as geographic location, family membership, practices, and living arrangements. The linkage, especially for children, between the individual and family environment is particularly crucial, and neither aspect should be seen in isolation. The Jewish religious variables utilized in this study reflect this linkage; for example, fasting is a personal decision and the rates of its occurrence can be counted individually. In contrast, candle lighting (Sabbath or Hanukkah) is a household practice, as is dietary observance (kashrut) in the home. The negotiation between individual and collective decisions is part of the process of socialization.

Data from our survey are available for up to twelve household members, but details on Jewishness, affiliation, etc., were collected for up to four children and up to four adults.[1] Therefore, to estimate the number of children participating in a particular activity, our statistics rely on children on whom we have data, rather than all the children in the surveyed households. For purposes of analysis, the child population has been divided into four age cohorts; 0–4, 5–9, 10–14, 15–17. Because of the three-year span of the final age cohort and the statistical unreliability when there are too few cases once these data are cross-tabulated with other variables, for some analysis we have collapsed the last two groups into a broader group, those aged 10–17.

We caution that the numbers for the Jewish population are estimates based upon a sample that has an overall 3 percent margin of error and a greater sampling error for subcategories. One other caveat needs stressing; we did not interview the children themselves. Rather, the respondents were adult household members, usually one of the parents, who answered on behalf of other adults and the children living in the household. Further, the respondents' answers reflect how they interpreted the questions. For example, if the respondent reported that his or her child had converted to Judaism, we accepted this answer and did not investigate the authenticity of this conversion.

Because NJPS data gathering took place in the spring and summer of 1990, it essentially provides a snapshot in time of American Jewry as it entered the last decade of the millennium. Therefore, we cannot talk about trends; this is a cross-sectional rather than a longitudinal study. Further, we do not know in sufficient detail about most earlier characteristics of the individuals or households. There is no claim made of causality. What produced a certain behavior or affiliation pattern can only be suggested or hinted at.

Unless, in response to a related question, the respondent provided specific information that he or she is the stepparent or adoptive parent of the child present, we assume that the children are the respondent's biological offspring. Except where noted, data provided in this report are based upon an unweighted sample that reflects the actual percentages determined by NJPS responses, e.g., percentage of children who lived in a home where Hanukkah candles are lit. Where we need to project an actual population, e.g., children presently receiving a Jewish education, we use weighted data. Nevertheless, because the size of the sample imposes certain limitations once cross-tabulations are made, we do not report on any characteristic when the number of cases in the particular cell are excessively low (e.g., Orthodox, single-parent households living in the West).

CHAPTER 2

THE DEMOGRAPHY OF THE JEWISH CHILD POPULATION

INTRODUCTION

This chapter assesses the demography[2] of the Jewish child population: How many children are there? What is their age and sex composition? Where do they reside? And what is the nature of their Jewishness—is it religious, ethnic, or cultural in nature? Later we will assess what impact these background elements have on the overall Jewish environment in which the children are raised and on Jewish continuity. For example, our analysis shows that the relatively low numbers of Jewish teenagers today is about to change. This could translate into a need for more Jewish youth group programs and Jewish community center activities. It could, in turn, mean more Jewish college students early in the new century.

The long history of the Jewish people has resulted in a complex web of Jewish self-identity and Jewish identification. Thus, Jewishness can take a number of different forms in a variety of settings—ethnic, religious, or cultural. Children are exposed to and influenced by the extent of the religious upbringing in their families, as well as by ethnic and cultural components reflecting the geographic origins of their ancestral families. Therefore, this research takes account of the Jewishness of the parents as well. As noted in chapter 1, the Core Jewish population of children consists of those identified by their parents in the survey as Jewish by religion, Jewish by choice, or as secular Jews, and whose parents did not ascribe to them any other ethno-religious identity. They may be Jews by religion or nonreligious cultural or secular Jews. They may be members of households that are entirely Jewish or mixed Jewish/non-Jewish, since a small number of households contain Jewish children but no Jewish adults (see note 4). Some Core Jewish children have a non-Jewish parent or stepparent, or possibly even a non-Jewish sibling. This demographic profile of the Jewish children first describes their age distribution and gender composition and compares them with those in the general white American population.[3] We then discuss the socio-demographic status of children and their families, where they live, and the Jewish identity of the children.

The children's demographic characteristics are affected greatly by the patterns of the parent generation. Most of the children in our sample have parents who were born in the baby boom years, 1945 until the mid-1960s. The entire U.S. child population grew substantially in those years, and so did the proportion of Jewish children. During the late 1960s and 1970s, when the baby boom generation of Jews reached adulthood, Jews married and produced offspring at lower rates than their parents and their non-Jewish peers. For this generation of Jews, higher education and career were greater priorities than starting a family. "The difference in overall fertility levels between Jewish and all U.S. white women is intimately linked with massive education differences. For women with a given education, fertility for Jewish and non-Jewish women age 25 and over is quite similar . . . within age groups, overall Jewish fertility (both 'children ever born' and 'percent childless' is systematically substantially below U.S. fertility, reflecting, of course, the highest proportion of Jewish women in the lower fertility, higher education categories. The Jewish women clearly delay or reduce their childbearing to a much greater degree than the non-Jewish women" (Mott and Abma 1992, 75). Moreover, these baby boomers, particularly the women, were more accepting of late marriage, in contrast to a more negative attitude toward late marriage in earlier generations. The degree to which Jewish women have outdistanced their non-Jewish counterparts in graduate and postgraduate education help to explain the delay in the age of marriage.

AGE DISTRIBUTION

Overall, the 1990 National Jewish Population Survey (NJPS) estimated the total NJPS child population to be 1,868,200 children age 0–17, living in all the qualified Jewish households, encompassed in the survey (the base here is the 8.1 million persons of all ages estimated in the total Jewish population). Thus children are 23 percent of the Total Jewish Population, both Core (Jewish by Religion or Jewish of No Religion) and non-Core (persons of Jewish background but not currently Jewish).

The age distribution of the total NJPS child population reveals a large base of 590,300 children under age 5, nearly 32 percent of the child population. We find a slightly smaller percentage in the age group 5–9. The older age group, 10–14, is smaller still, with only 487,300 children, or 26 percent of all children. This decline is explained by either fewer children per couple in the 1975–1980 birth cohort, or by the size of the age cohorts of mothers discussed later in this chapter. The post–World War II baby boom generation tended to marry later than their parents and did not begin to produce significant numbers of children until the 1980s.

DEMOGRAPHIC PROFILE BY CATEGORY OF JEWISHNESS

Of the 1.87 million Jewishly connected children identified in the U.S. population, according to the NJPS respondents' replies, nearly 845,000 were born Jewish and are thus called Born Jews: Religion Judaism (BJR). More than 11,000 children are themselves Jews by Choice, namely converts to Judaism (JBC), according to their parents. Thus the total number of children who are Jewish by Religion (JBR) is about 856,000. An additional 307,000 children are secular Jews, not currently identified as Jewish by religion, but considered by their families culturally Jewish (JNR). Collectively, these two groups, (JBR and JNR) comprise the Core Jewish child population, which approximates 1,163,000 (see Table 2.1).

Table 2.1 Total NJPS Child Population and Core Jewish Children 0–17 by Age
(weighted data) (Sample: N=1489)

Age Group	Core Jewish Population	Percentage	Total NJPS Child Population	Percentage	Total U.S. White Population	Percentage
0–4	391,300	33.6	590,300	31.6	13,649,000	28.4
5–9	360,600	31.0	571,400	30.6	13,617,000	28.3
10–14	270,300	23.2	487,300	26.1	12,854,000	26.7
15–17	140,600	12.1	219,200	11.7	8,006,000	16.6
Total	1,163,000	100.0	1,868,200	100.0	48,126,000	100.0

The remaining group in the Total NJPS child population consists of children
being raised in a religion other than Judaism. We refer to these as JCOR (Jewish Children Other Religion). They comprise 38 percent of the overall child population (Figure 2.2). This population includes some children being raised in two religions, Judaism and some other religion; they number approximately 707,000.[4] Slightly more
than 16 percent of all children are Jewish with No Religion (JNR). If we focus just on
the Core Jewish child population, we note that more than one quarter (26.3 percent)
are classified as having no religion, with the remaining three-quarters Jewish by Religion (JBR).

Thousands (weighted data)

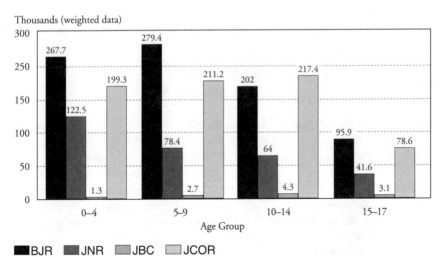

BJR: Born Jewish and Jewish by Religion = 845,000. JNR: Jews with no religion = 307,000
JBC: Jews by choice = 11,000. Total Core Jewish Child Population = 1,163,000
JCOR: Children With Other Religion = 707,000. Total NJPS Child Population = 1,868,000

Figure 2.1 Total NJPS Child Population: Age by Category of Jewishness

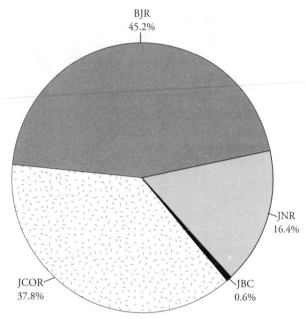

BJR = Born Jewish and Jewish religion; JNR = Jewish with no religion; JBC = Jewish by choice; JCOR = Children of Jewish background with other religion

Figure 2.2 Total Jewishly Connected Child Population by Category of Jewishness

AGE DISTRIBUTION BY CATEGORY
OF JEWISHNESS

The age distribution (Figure 2.1) suggests that the proportion of all Jewish children who are secular, that is, Jewish with no religion, has increased dramatically in the past decade. Nearly a third of all Core Jewish children age 0–4 are identified by their parents as Jewish but are being raised with no religion, as compared to only 22 percent of those age 5–9, and 24 percent of children 10–17. One-fifth of the total Core Jewish population (including adults) were identified as having no religion. The majority of the Jewishly identified children being raised in no religion are the children of interfaith couples.

Approximately 42 percent of children age 10–17 in the total NJPS child population would be considered JCOR; however, only 35 percent of children under 10 fit into this category. This could reflect a tendency to shift out of the "no religion" category to "another religion" category once the child approaches the teen years.

AGE DISTRIBUTION OF THE CORE JEWISH CHILD
POPULATION IN COMPARISON WITH
THE WHITE U.S. CHILD POPULATION

In the United States, out of a total white population of 200 million persons in 1990, 48 million, or 24 percent, were under age 18 (U.S Census, 1990: Vol. 1, Ch. 13). For the NJPS Core Jewish population, only 21 percent, or 1.16 million of the 5.51 million total Core Jewish population, fall into this younger age cohort. This is because "Jews in the United States have long been characterized by a relatively older population. Reflecting the combined effects of lower fertility and the growing concentration of the large number of immigrants from the early 1900s among the aged, the Core Jewish population continues to be older than the white population of the U.S. (The difference is even greater when non-whites are included)" (Goldstein 1992, 105).

Within the past decade, however, the Jewish population has shown signs of reversing the pattern. Young Jews make up the same proportion of the overall Jewish population as their corresponding cohorts do in the overall white population (Figure 2.3).

U.S. white children age 0–9 are 13.6 percent of the total white population. This is the same as the proportion of Jews in that age group, but Jews have slightly fewer in the 5–9 group and slightly more in the 0–4 category. This suggests that in the decade

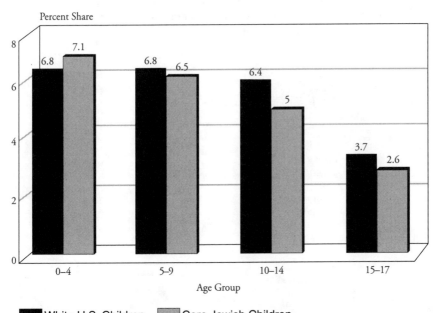

■■■White U.S. Children   ▨Core Jewish Children
Total U.S. White Child Population = 47,597,000
Total Core Jewish Child Population = 1,163,000
Based upon the 1990 NJPS and U.S. Census

Figure 2.3 Child Population by Age: Percent Share of Total Core Jewish and White U.S. Populations

1980–1990 Jewish children were being born at a rate similar to that for all American whites, possibly reflecting a narrowing of earlier differentials between Jews and whites generally. By contrast, children age 10–17 in the Core Jewish population constitute 7.6 percent of the Core Jewish population of all ages compared to white children age 10–17 constituting 10.1 percent of the 200 million persons in the total white population. The upswing in Jewish births in the 1980s may only be a temporary effect due to the timing of births. Given past differences, it seems unlikely to reflect an increase in the total Jewish fertility rate, that is, the overall number of children born to each woman.

SEX RATIOS OF CORE JEWISH CHILDREN

Core Jews under age 18 are characterized by a sex ratio of 109 males per 100 females (see Table 2.2). The sex ratio in the age group 0–4 is 106, in the smaller age 5–9 category it is 116, and it returns to 106 for Jews age 10–17.

In the U.S. white child population there is a sex ratio of 105 males per 100 females. For the U.S. white child population, the higher male ratio is relatively consistent, extending across each age cohort at either 105 or 106.

The fluctuations in the sex ratio for the Jewish child population, as opposed to the greater consistency in the general child population numbers, may be explained by the smaller size of the Jewish population sample.

Table 2.2 U.S. and Core Jewish Child Populations by Age and Sex Ratio
(weighted data)

	Core Jewish Child Population		
Age Group	*Male*	*Female*	*Sex Ratio M/F × 100*
0–4	201,000	190,000	106
5–9	194,000	167,000	116
10–17	211,000	200,000	106
Total	606,000	557,000	109

	U.S. White Child Population*		
Age Group	*Male*	*Female*	*Sex Ratio*
0–4	7,004,000	6,645,000	105
5–9	6,991,000	6,626,000	105
10–17	10,715,000	10,145,000	106
Total	24,710,000	23,416,000	105

*Source: Statistical Abstract 1992, "1990 Resident Population by Age and Race–Table 18."

GEOGRAPHIC DISTRIBUTION AND CATEGORY OF JEWISHNESS BY CENSUS REGION

Regional distribution, stemming largely from internal migration patterns of the American Jewish population, is closely tied to demographic, social, and economic variables that affect the individual's ties to the larger Jewish community. American Jews have always been a highly mobile people. This presents challenges to individuals and to the national Jewish community.

Goldstein and Goldstein (1996, 261) point out that, "these patterns point to considerably lower levels of involvement in the [Jewish] community of the more mobile segment, especially those under age 45. They suggest that migration, either as a selective process or by disrupting the usual linkages of individuals and families to the community's organized structure, is associated with lesser integration of migrants into the Jewish community." High levels of mobility and geographic dispersion impact heavily on the cultural, social, and religious vitality of the Jewish community. Because Jewish Americans tend to be highly educated and thus have enhanced career opportunities, they enjoy a vast freedom of choice about where to live. Attraction to better climates, leisure time activities, and cultural centers also motivate Jews and others to relocate. This often means movement out of centers of Jewish concentration, such as the Northeast and older metropolitan areas elsewhere. It has resulted in increased opportunities for interactions with non-Jews. Jewish institutions in some older communities have dwindled as the socio-religious functions they performed have diminished; they are not always reestablished in the newer areas of settlement, especially if the population is more dispersed. And where Jewish communal organizations have been recreated in the new communities, they often do not generate the old loyalties.

Geographic mobility combines positive and negative features for the Jewish community. Positively, there is more freedom associated with migration, yielding greater innovation as the result of interaction with people from a variety of backgrounds. The negative effect is social isolation, exemplified by a breakdown in family life, the loss of a sense of community, and a society in which people know little and understand little about each other (Goldstein and Goldstein 1996). As for children, mobility means transferring to new schools and establishing new friendships, which may hamper Jewish socialization and connections to the Jewish community, especially if the new residence is in locations with lower Jewish density.

For all of these reasons it is important to identify where Jewish children live and what redistribution patterns they are experiencing. In doing so we need to keep in mind that children usually live with their parents and mobility is most commonly based on parental decisions.

Of the total NJPS child population of 1.87 million children—both Core Jewish children and children of Jewish background not now Jewish (JCOR)—37 percent live in the Northeast, 27 percent in the West, 23 percent in the South, and slightly less than 13 percent in the Midwest (see Map 2.1).

NJPS data indicate that the Northeast not only has a much greater number of Core Jewish children than any other region of the United States (see Map 2.1), but it

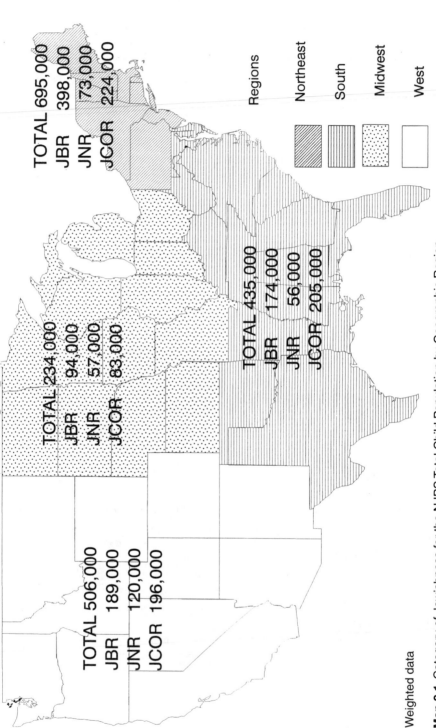

TOTAL 695,000
JBR 398,000
JNR 73,000
JCOR 224,000

TOTAL 234,000
JBR 94,000
JNR 57,000
JCOR 83,000

TOTAL 435,000
JBR 174,000
JNR 56,000
JCOR 205,000

TOTAL 506,000
JBR 189,000
JNR 120,000
JCOR 196,000

Regions

Northeast

South

Midwest

West

Weighted data

Map 2.1 Category of Jewishness for the NJPS Total Child Population by Geographic Region

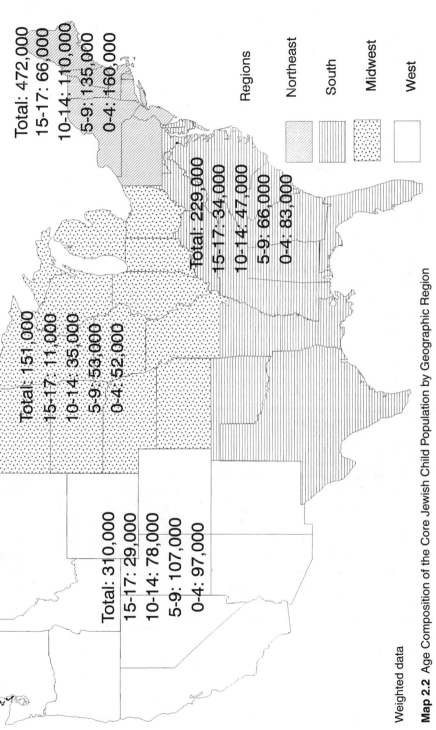

Total: 472,000
15-17: 66,000
10-14: 110,000
5-9: 135,000
0-4: 160,000

Total: 151,000
15-17: 11,000
10-14: 35,000
5-9: 53,000
0-4: 52,000

Total: 310,000
15-17: 29,000
10-14: 78,000
5-9: 107,000
0-4: 97,000

Total: 229,000
15-17: 34,000
10-14: 47,000
5-9: 66,000
0-4: 83,000

Regions

Northeast

South

Midwest

West

Weighted data

Map 2.2 Age Composition of the Core Jewish Child Population by Geographic Region

is also the region that has the largest proportion of its Core Jewish child population who are Jewish by Religion (JBR) as opposed to Jewish with no Religion (JNR). Over 84 percent of that region's Core Jewish children are JBR. In the South, slightly more than three-quarters (76 percent) of the Core Jewish children are JBR, and in both the Midwest and the West just over 60 percent of Core Jewish children are JBR.

Nearly half of the nation's 856,000 children who are Jewish by Religion (JBR) live in the Northeast. This is followed by the West at 22 percent, and the South at just over 20 percent. The Midwest contains only 11 percent of the nation's children who are JBR.

If we include the JNR children along with those who are JBR, we find that of the total Core Jewish population nearly 41 percent live in the Northeast. Close to 27 percent reside in the West, nearly 20 percent in the South and just 13 percent in the Midwest.

Geographic analysis of NJPS data indicates that most measures of Jewish practice and behavior (for instance synagogue membership, observing the dietary laws, giving to Jewish causes) are highest in the Northeast. This could well reflect the higher intermarriage rates in the regions outside the Northeast as well as community patterns that are less conducive to a more involved Jewish lifestyle. For example, a certain Jewish population density is necessary to support Jewish schools, kosher facilities, Jewish organizations, and other institutions that facilitate a high degree of Jewish practice, behavior, and culture. Regional cultural and lifestyle differences could also affect the motivation to participate in community organizations. It may well be that the marginal or less Jewishly connected Jewish families have a greater propensity to migrate and leave areas of intensive Jewish settlement such as the Northeast, though we cannot prove this due to the limitations of NJPS.

In fact, the Northeast is the dominant region of residence for Core Jews in all age categories. Comparing the Jewish child population to the Jewish population of all ages, we find that around 45 percent of the U.S. Core Jewish population live in the Northeast, as do close to 41 percent of Core Jewish children. This differential in the proportion of children in the Northeast is reversed in the West. Only 21 percent of the Core Jewish population lives in the western United States, compared to nearly 27 percent of the under-18 Core Jewish population. Like the Northeast, the South also includes a smaller share of the Core Jewish child population than it does for the total Jewish population. The pattern in the South can be understood by noting the large number of Jewish elderly who have migrated to the region after World War II. The West has had a similarly large migration, but it has been more characterized by younger adults and many families with children. For example, in 1990, 17 percent of the Jews in the West were age 65 and over, compared to 21 percent in the South.

DEMOGRAPHIC TRENDS OF THE JEWISH CHILD POPULATION

As discussed earlier, over the last generation, many Jews have delayed marriage until their midtwenties or later. In 1990 Jewish women aged 35–44 had first married on av-

Table 2.3 Average Age of Jewish Parents by Age of Youngest Child in NJPS Sample[5] (N=1002)

Age of Youngest Child in 1990	Age of Father in 1990	Age of Father at Child's Birth*	Age of Mother in 1990	Age of Mother at Child's Birth*
0–4	36	34	33	31
5–9	38	31	36	29
10–14	41	29	39	27
15–17	43	27	41	25
Average Age	39	—	37	—

*Computed for middle point in age bracket.

erage at age 24.2 compared with 22.0 among those 45–64 (Goldstein 1992, 165). By the late 1970s and continuing into the 1980s and early 1990s, most of the Jewish baby boomers began to marry and produce more children. As shown in Table 2.3, we note that they became parents at later ages than in the recent past. The sociological changes that contributed to their earlier delay were now leading to a higher number of Jewish children being born during the 1980s.

We realize that the increased number of children may reflect nothing more than delayed fertility, rather than larger families. Thus, the late start of family formation also implies that relatively few mothers will produce more than two children. Nevertheless, this concentration of births in a short time period impacts the age "pyramid." The "baby boomlet" of the late 1980s is reflected in the larger sizes of age groups 0–4 and 5–9 among Jewish children compared to the teenage cohorts.

Determinants of higher fertility for Jews in the 1980s include both biological and sociological factors. It is probable that many Jewish women born during the first half of the baby boom years became more aware of their biological "clocks" during the 1980s and thus decided to begin having children, thereby leading to relatively large numbers of children overall during the 1980s. This is demonstrated in Table 2.3. The average age at which mothers of children 0–4 in 1990 had their first child is 31 and for fathers it is 34. By contrast, those whose youngest children are now age 15–17 had their first child at ages 25 and 27 respectively, for mothers and fathers, which is six to seven years younger. Moreover, one would expect increases in the age of parents commensurate with the intervals of ages for the children; a ten year differential would be expected for the oldest parents compared to the youngest parents. Instead, the increases are less. For example, Jewish fathers of 15–17 year old children are only seven years older on average than the fathers of 0–4 year olds, and mothers of 15–17 year old children are only eight years older than mothers of 0–4 year olds. Overall for Jewish parents with children under 18, the average age is 39 for Jewish fathers and 37 for Jewish mothers. The implications of these data suggest that those couples who choose to become parents at older ages also tend to have shorter spacing between the births of their children.

SUMMARY

In recent decades there have been significant changes in the age composition, Jewish identity, and geographical location of the child population. A key demographic finding of the 1990 NJPS is the rise in the number of babies being born in the 1980s, yielding a substantial "baby boomlet." Overall, in 1990 there were many more Core Jewish children in the younger age cohorts (0–9) than in the older age groupings (10–17), even accounting for the fact that the first age group consists of ten years and the later has only eight years. As a whole, American Jews are significantly older than U.S. whites, yet 7.1 percent of all Jews are in ages 0–4, slightly above the 6.8 percent of all white Americans who are in this youngest age group. The consequences of a larger cohort of children following a period of population bust poses major planning challenges. The size of the classes entering all levels of Jewish educational institutions and recreational programs will be larger than those graduating. This will create greater demand for teachers and youth workers, along with greater financial expenditures, and require more physical facilities and plant if the community wishes to maintain and even to increase levels of participation.

In addition, a substantial rise has occurred in the proportion of Core Jewish children who are of no religion—close to one-third of those in ages 0–4. This large secularly oriented child population poses a further challenge to Jewish communal institutions interested in outreach. Furthermore, population redistribution across the United States has major implications for community planning and resources. While the Northeast has the largest number of Jewish children, the West is of growing importance, since it has a larger proportional share of the nation's Jewish children than of the adult population. These findings call for a national reassessment of needs and requirements in the allocation of child-related services by the Jewish community.

CHAPTER 3

THE IMPACT OF
HOME BACKGROUND
ON THE SOCIALIZATION
OF CHILDREN

INTRODUCTION

To sustain itself as a viable and distinct entity, the Jewish community must socialize Jewish children into Jewish identity.[6] The formation of a specifically Jewish identity has its roots in the home. Values must be transmitted from one generation to the next to maintain cultural continuity (Hoge et al. 1982). As Chaim Waxman states: "Certainly within the history and tradition of Jews, the family has been the most prominent institution involved in ethno-religious identity formation and the transmission of ethno-religious norms and values" (1983, 160).

The research described here explores the various factors that help produce effectively socialized Jewish children and thereby to enhance Jewish continuity. In doing so, we also examine factors involving the larger society, especially since the changing character of the American family is reflected in the Jewish family as well. This traditional family and parenting structure has long been regarded as a bulwark ensuring the stability of Jewish society. According to Waxman: "The main structural component of Jewish communal life is the two-parent family and there is a dialectical relationship between the structure and the religious-cultural value of the centrality of that family form" (1983, 165). But as we know, these family types are not as prevalent today.

This chapter on household composition explores the role of different home settings in the social and economic status of children. First, we describe the variety of settings involving contemporary Jewish children. Second, we compare children's patterns of general education: whether they go to a private or a public school, to a Jewish or a non-Jewish school. Further, we examine the extent and depth of any Jewish education the children may have received. Family participation in the Jewish community will also be examined by attention to membership in synagogues, voluntarism, and philanthropic behavior. The central hypothesis is that household composition is strongly associated with the economic and social welfare of children. Moreover, as we will see, household composition is also related to the religious, cultural, and ethnic socialization of children.

HOUSEHOLD STRUCTURE: COMPARATIVE DATA OF THE JEWISH AND U.S WHITE CHILD POPULATIONS[7]

Two-Parent Households

Overwhelmingly, today Jewish children live with their parents. Table 3.1 displays the number of Core Jewish children by household type, weighted to reflect actual population numbers. It shows that 78 percent of the children live with their parents and no other adults. Nearly 7 percent of the children are living with both parents and other adults, either relatives or non-relatives. The two-parent household structure is by far the most common type for all white American children (79 percent, according to the 1990 U.S. Census); for Jewish children this pattern is even more pronounced. As Table 3.1 indicates, about 85 percent (78.0 + 6.6) of Jewish children are raised in this type of family structure. This suggests that the Jewish family is very stable and still follows conventional patterns. As we will demonstrate, this traditional family structure has positive consequences on the socio-economic well-being of children.

Single-Parent Households: Comparative Data

Nearly 4 percent of the 2.68 million NJPS Core Jewish households qualify as single-parent households. However, of the 761,000 households with children, about 12.5 percent consist of a single parent. In about 59 percent of these single-parent households, children live with only a single parent. The remaining 41 percent of these households also contain other adults present, either family or nonfamily. From the

Table 3.1 Number of Core Jewish Children by Age and Household Composition
(weighted data with percentages in parenthesis)

Children by Household Composition	Age of Children				Total # of of children
	0–4 N=321	5–9 N=304	10–14 N=243	15–17 N=134	N=1002
Couple N=817	332,300 (84.4)	285,500 (79.2)	193,800 (71.7)	95,200 (67.7)	906,900 (78.0)
Couple + Other Adults N=62	19,600 (5.0)	25,300 (7.0)	23,800 (8.8)	8,500 (6.0)	77,100 (6.6)
Single-parent N=62	13,900 (3.6)	24,200 (6.7)	26,800 (9.9)	19,300 (13.7)	84,100 (7.2)
Single-parent + Others N=39	16,400 (4.2)	19,300 (5.4)	18,700 (6.9)	14,200 (10.1)	68,500 (5.9)
Non-Normative N=22	9,100 (2.3)	6,400 (1.8)	7,300 (2.7)	3,400 (2.4)	26,200 (2.3)
Total N=1002	391,300 (100.0)	360,500 (100.0)	270,300 (100.0)	140,700 (100.0)	1,162,800 (100.0)

perspective of the children, the data show that about 13 percent of all Core Jewish children live in single-parent households, as compared with 19 percent of white American children. Just over 7 percent of Core Jewish children live in households with single parents and no other adults, and nearly 6 percent live in households with a single parent and other adults, as indicated in Table 3.1.

For the U.S. population, the proportion of single-parent families has significantly increased over the past generation. In 1970, 11.1 percent of white family households were single-parent, while in 1990 this proportion was 17.0 percent (Statistical Abstract 1993, 56). We assume that the same trend probably applies to Jews, although we lack historical data. Traditionally, it was poor, nonwhite, uneducated, and unemployed women who were most likely to be single parents. There is evidence that this profile has changed somewhat: "While their numbers are still small, the most dramatic increases [in single-parent families between 1982 and 1992] were found among whites (a rise from about 6.7 percent to 14.6 percent), college graduates (from 3.0 percent to 6.4 percent), and women in professional and managerial jobs (from 3.1 percent to 8.3 percent)" (Seligmann and Hamilton 1993, 53). This pattern could reflect changing family structures, a redefining of the place of marriage in our society, and the advancement of women in educational attainment leading to postponement of marriage. At the same time, middle-class acceptance of unwed mothers has grown, and single-parent families are less likely to be considered social outcasts.

Non-Normative Households

The non-normative households described here may be an unmarried couple, a gay or lesbian couple, or other unrelated adults with children present. As lifestyles have diversified in the latter half of the twentieth century, there are many variations in household structure and in relationships between individuals within these non-normative households. The non-normative designation does not reflect a value judgment. It is simply a description that sets a particular household type apart from the more common married-couple households.

Around 2 percent of the households in our sample with children are defined as non-normative. We can project that slightly more than 26,000 Core Jewish children live in over 14,000 households that can be described this way. According to the 1990 U.S. Census, slightly less than 2 percent of American children do not live with their parents but rather with relatives or another nonrelated guardian. In NJPS, only six households were found with children who do not live with a parent, but reside with relatives or another guardian. Those six households representing under one percent of the sample are excluded from the analyses where parents' traits are being studied in relation to their children's upbringing.

JEWISH SINGLE-PARENT HOUSEHOLD PATTERNS

As indicated by the comparative data on child population by age (Table 3.1), with increasing age there is a shift away from the traditional pattern of both parents living with their children. Older children are more likely than younger children to live with a single parent, usually their mother. We can attribute this trend to demographic factors, primarily the increased incidence of divorce as children get older. Even though the proportion of children under 5 in one-parent families is smaller than among 15–17 year-olds, we find that in absolute numbers there are nearly as many young children as teenagers in such families. This is one result of the demographic baby boomlet of recent years (reflected in Table 3.1), which reveals more younger children than older children in the Jewish population.

For the single-parent households in NJPS, 71.8 percent were headed by the mother of the child(ren) and 28.2 percent were headed by the father. Among the overall U.S. white population, the tendency for the mother to head a single-parent household was even greater (84.4 percent); only 15.6 percent were headed by a father. Both U.S. Census data and NJPS information indicate that single-parent households in which the father is the parent are much better off economically than mother-headed single-parent households (Statistical Abstract 1992, 54).

The distribution of children within the single-parent category (Table 3.2) according to the marital status of the single parent shows that most of the children live with either a divorced (35 percent) or separated (26 percent) parent. Almost 22 percent live with a never-married parent. We did not ask of parents in this never-married group if they were "single parents by choice." Like their counterparts nationwide, only a small portion (9 percent) of Jewish children under age 18 who are in single-parent households live with a widowed parent, while another 9 percent live with a parent who is still married but whose spouse is absent. The comparison to the general population reveals that among Jews a lower percentage of single parents are divorced, but a higher percentage are separated. Collectively, the proportion of divorced and separated single parents is roughly equivalent in the two populations. In both the U.S. white and NJPS populations, the likelihood for children to be in a single-parent household increases as the child gets older, as the effects of divorce, separation, and widowhood increase.

Table 3.2 Children Living with One-Parent by Marital Status of Parent*,
Core Jews and U.S. Whites (in percentages)

Marital Status of Parent	NJPS*	U.S. Whites**
Married, spouse absent	9.2	3.8
Never Married	21.7	19.2
Divorced	35.0	49.1
Separated	25.6	20.1
Widowed	8.6	7.8
Total	100.0	100.0

*NJPS weighted data (N=129); **white population, U.S. Census, 1990.

PARENTAL MARRIAGE PATTERNS AND CUSTODY ARRANGEMENTS

Figure 3.1 graphically presents the child population by age and by marital status of the parent(s) with whom they live. About 160,000 or 16 percent of Core Jewish children in a two-parent household live with a parent who had remarried and a stepparent. The likelihood is greatest amongst households with older children, as more years have elapsed in which marriage dissolution and remarriage could occur. Thus, just 12.8 percent of young children 0–4 live in a household with a remarried parent, while 17.8 percent of adolescents, children age 15–17, do so.

Attention to divorce or separation as related to intermarriage shows that among Jewish parents divorced or separated from a non-Jewish spouse who have children under 18, 44.6 percent have sole custody, 18.1 percent have joint custody, 33.7 percent have no custody, and the remaining 3.6 percent have some other arrangement. Again, the majority of Jewish parents have either sole or joint custody of the children, potentially enabling them to maintain Jewish identity.

In terms of the sex of the custodial parent among marriages that have resulted in divorce or separation, 82 percent of mothers received full custody, 5 percent joint custody, 11 percent do not have custody, and 2 percent had some other arrangement.

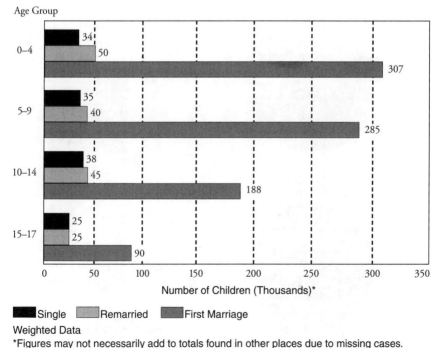

Age Group

Number of Children (Thousands)*

■ Single ▨ Remarried ▦ First Marriage
Weighted Data
*Figures may not necessarily add to totals found in other places due to missing cases.

Figure 3.1 Core Jewish Child Population by Marital Status of Their Parents

For fathers, nearly 17 percent received sole custody, 27 percent joint custody, half had no custody, and 6 percent had some other arrangement. By comparison many more Jewish fathers have joint or sole custody of their children after divorce than the U.S. norm. Among all U.S. households that experienced divorce, only 9 percent of fathers received full custody, 16 percent got joint custody, 72 percent were not given any custody, and 3 percent had some other arrangement (National Center for Health Statistics, Table 17, 1995). This suggests that Jewish men place more importance on their parental role. Their above-average socio-economic status and financial resources probably help them fulfill their role as fathers.

Figure 3.2 displays information on the marital status of parents of Core Jewish children. The overwhelming majority of Jewish fathers (93.7 percent) are currently married, while 2.4 percent are divorced and a similar percentage separated. The remaining small proportions are either widowed or have never married. For Jewish mothers, 85 percent are currently married, 2.5 percent are separated, and 9.3 percent are divorced. For the remaining single mothers, 1.8 percent were never married and 1.4 percent are widowed.

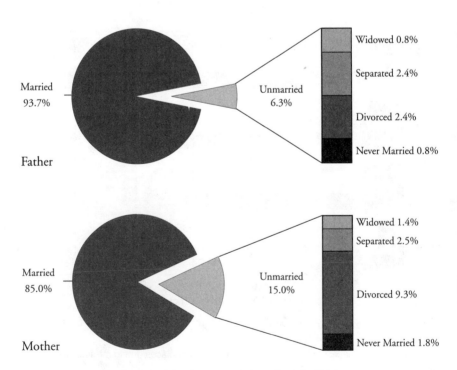

Figure 3.2 Marital Status of the Parents of Core Jewish Children

NON-NORMATIVE HOUSEHOLD PATTERNS

Since the NJPS sample provided only twenty-two cases of children under age 18 living in non-normative families, we have excluded those children from any multilevel analyses. However, it is worth observing that children in non-normative households appear to be spread evenly across the age categories, unlike children in single-parent families, who tend to be older. Perhaps the non-normative pattern is a lifestyle choice of the parents unrelated to marriage breakups.

HOUSEHOLD COMPOSITION AND PER CAPITA INCOME

The 1990 U.S. Census indicated that increasing proportions of children are living in households below the poverty line, and that most of these children belong to single-parent families. There is a clear relation between poverty and single-parenthood. In 1990 the Census Bureau reported that 47 percent of the families headed by single mothers lived in poverty, as against 8.3 percent of the families headed by two parents (*New York Times* 1993, A–14). The poverty level for a family of four established by the Office of Management and Budget for 1989 (the period in which NJPS respondents reported their yearly household income) was $12,675 a year (U.S. Bureau of the Census, Current Population Reports, P-60, No. 175). Indeed the 1990 Census data show that while the average annual income for families with children in two-parent households was $50,000, in single-mother households the average annual income dropped below $20,000. In single-father households, which are less common, income level was higher, approximately $27,000.

NJPS found that of Core Jewish households with children (which average nearly four persons per household), approximately 3 percent—23,000 households—earn less than $12,675 annually. This means that about 34,000 Jewish children are living below the national poverty level. If we define low-income households with children as those earning less than $20,000, we find that 6.7 percent, close to 51,000 Core Jewish households containing about 77,000 children, are low-income. Approximately 68 percent of Core Jewish households with children earn between $20,000 and $80,000 annually and about one quarter earn more than $80,000. Our data show rather clearly that the Jewish households are better off economically than American households overall. However, those 77,000 Jewish children living below the poverty line or in low-income categories are clearly vulnerable from a Jewish communal perspective. Thus for financial reasons they are less likely to have access to private Jewish education or other fee-paying Jewish institutions.

Overall, the average household income for Jewish families with children in 1989 was $63,900, far above the national average of $34,600 for families with children (1991 Statistical Abstract, 450). Table 3.3 shows that household income ranged from nearly $70,000 in households where there were two parents and another adult, down to $35,600 where there was only a single parent. A more accurate assessment of affluence is per capita income in households containing Jewish children under 18, which was $20,400 in 1990.[8] There is a clear link between marital status and income.

Table 3.3   Household Composition and Income in 1989 in Core Jewish Households with
             Children Age 0–17

Household Composition	Per Capita Income	Household Income
Couple	$20,800	$66,000
Couple + Others	$20,500	$69,900
Single Parent	$16,600	$35,600
Single Parent + Others	$16,900	$39,400
Total Households (N=896)	$20,400	$63,900

As with American children in general, Jewish children are economically better off living in a household with two parents. Per capita income in households with children
who live with both a father and mother was $20,800 in 1990, compared to only
$16,600 for children in households with only one parent, as indicated in Table 3.3.

The small number of households containing both parents and others (relatives
or nonrelatives) have a slightly lower per capita income of $20,500, but that is higher
than the income level in single-parent households with other members—$16,900
—and also higher than the $16,600 income for single-parent households with no other
members.

Household income is an indicator of economic status and level of living in the
United States. This socioeconomic environment shapes the lifestyle options available
to any American family. For example, a family with a high income may choose to send
the children to private schools. They can also afford to enrich family life with after-
school programs, summer camp, a health club, or other facilities providing special activities for children, such as sports, art, and music. High income, then, can be used as
a proxy for well-being.

Living Jewishly

Involvement in Jewish life and the organized community generally requires significant
sums of money: to join a synagogue or Jewish community center (JCC), to send the
children to supplementary Hebrew school or Jewish day school, to visit Israel, to go
to Jewish summer camp or join a Jewish youth group, and to celebrate a Bar/Bat Mitzvah. Given a parental commitment to Jewish socialization, children in households
with a higher per capita income not only are given more options to enrich their life,
but also more opportunity to develop, bond, and connect with their heritage, and become more involved with the Jewish community. For example, Lipset found that only
28 percent of parents with family income under $40,000 have children that are at-
tending or will be attending a Jewish educational program, while 41 percent of those
earning more than $80,000 do (1993).

But income is not the only factor affecting intensity of Jewish involvement. In his research on the cost of living Jewishly, Winter cautions that, "The decision of whether or not to affiliate with a synagogue or to make a relatively high contribution to a Federation campaign, is not solely a consequence of family income. The level of Jewish identity or commitment is also related to a family's determination of whether a given aspect of living Jewishly is or is not affordable; that is whether or not a given Jewish activity or affiliation is regarded as affordable is apt to be dependent both on family income or discretionary funds and on the degree of Jewish identity or commitment" (Winter 1989, 149).

Number of Children

As Table 3.4 indicates, there is a relationship between household income and presence of children. For the Core Jewish households headed by adults ages 18–44 (the cohort most likely to include children), just 7 percent earn less than $20,000 and 10.5 percent earn more than $125,000. The data show a slight tendency for larger families to have more income. Possibly the higher-income families are more established, and the earners are older and have been married longer. Second, in a largely middle-class population that efficiently uses family planning, there is a tendency to have children only when financially affordable. Households with no children are overrepresented in the low-income category. However, this may reflect lack of time and opportunity to complete education and to raise a family.

Table 3.4 Annual Household Income in 1989 by Number of Children for Core Jewish Adults Age 18–44 (in percentages)

	Number of Children				
Income Category	*0*	*1*	*2*	*3 or more*	*Total*
Under $20,000 N=74	10.0	2.9	5.4	2.3	7.0
$20,000–$39,999 N=242	24.9	23.0	17.6	25.0	23.0
$40,000–$59,999 N=274	24.7	24.5	30.6	26.1	26.0
$60,000–$79,999 N=181	13.9	22.5	19.8	18.2	17.2
$80,000–$124,999 N=171	16.0	19.6	14.9	13.6	16.2
$125,000+ N=111	10.6	7.4	11.7	14.8	10.5
Total % of households	100.0	100.0	100.0	100.0	100.0
Number	N=539	N=204	N=222	N=88	N=1053

WORKING MOTHERS AND HOUSEHOLD
COMPOSITION

Dual-earner couples have become increasingly common—63 percent of U. S. women are now working outside their household (Characteristics of the Civilian Labor Force 1989, Chart 636, U.S. Bureau of Labor Statistics). This reflects both the higher proportion of women who obtain higher education and are professionally trained, and the need for many families to have a second income in order to achieve sufficient household income. The percentage of mothers who work outside the home for pay has increased steadily over the past generation. In 1987, 53 percent of married mothers with children age one and under were in the labor force, which was more than double the 24 percent rate in 1970 (U.S. Bureau of Labor Statistics 1987). The rate in 1989 of maternal employment for two-parent families with schoolchildren was 71 percent (Hoffman 1989, 283). Employment patterns of mothers vary according to the age of the youngest child, the woman's educational level, age, and income level of the husband, and place of residence.

What is the impact of working mothers on the well-being of children? It depends on many variables, such as the age of the children and the type of child care available. Research on this subject reveals diverse opinions. One late 1970s study found, "children of mothers who were not employed vocalized more to their mothers. Additionally there were more reciprocal social interactions between nonemployed mothers and their children" (Cohen 1978, 193). This author adds, "The children whose mothers were not employed scored higher on the Bayley Mental Scale and on the Gesell Development Schedule at 24 months" (Cohen 1978, 194). But other studies come to different conclusions: "Employment can enhance a woman's life, providing stimulation, self-esteem, adult contacts, escape from repetitive routines of housework and child care and a buffer against stress from family roles. . . . a mother's satisfaction with her employment status relates positively to the quality of the mother-child interaction and also to the various indexes of the child's adjustment and abilities" (Hoffman 1989, 284).

Table 3.5 shows the employment status of Jewish mothers by household composition. Overall, 67 percent of the mothers are working outside the home, a substantial majority of them full-time. Only a small proportion of the rest of these women are unemployed or students (7 percent); 26 percent define themselves as homemakers. Comparing working patterns by household composition we find some differences. Although single mothers are only somewhat more likely to be employed than mothers in two-parent families (71 percent vs. 67 percent), 48 percent of the former work full-time, as opposed to 38 percent of the latter. We can assume that economic necessity is a stronger determinant of single mothers' working patterns because of their exclusive responsibility as the sole parent. However, small cell sizes preclude appropriate comparison.

Labor-force participation of mothers varies by age of their youngest child. "Participation rates for women in the 'prime' working age groups (25–44) have been increasing steadily and consistently, and the rates for married women with school-age children (6–17) have been remarkably similar to the rates for all women" (Chiswick

Table 3.5 Employment Status of Mothers in Core Jewish Households by Household
Composition

Household Composition	Employment Status of Mothers in Percentages				
	Full-Time	*Part-Time*	*Homemaker*	*Unemployed*	*Total*
Couple N=441	38	29	28	5	100
Couple + Others N=34	44	23	26	6	100
Single Parent N=31	48	23	3	26	100
Single Parent + Others N=15	47	7	7	39	100
Total HHs N=521	39	28	26	7	100

1994, 6). In her report, Chiswick also indicates that 75.6 percent of married adult
Jewish women with children age 6–17 are currently employed, in contrast to the 49.4
percent of women with children under 6. Both of these percentages have increased
dramatically since 1957, when the figures stood at 28.6 percent and 11.8 percent respectively.

NJPS data indicate that Jewish mothers are much less likely than the general
population to work full-time when their youngest child is under the age of 5 (see Table
3.6). This reflects a cultural preference for parental child rearing of infants and toddlers and also reflects greater economic freedom not to work, i.e., greater income. The
proportion of full-time employment of these mothers increases from 34 percent when
the youngest child is age 0–4 to 52 percent where the child is over age 14. At the same
time, part-time employment decreases from 26 percent to 19 percent. In chapter 6
we will discuss child-care arrangements and the Jewish communal response to these
issues.

Table 3.6 Employment Status of Mothers by Age of Youngest Child in Two-Parent
Households with Core Jewish Children (in percentages)

Employment Status of the Mother	Age of the Youngest Child in Percentages				*AVERAGE*
	0–4	*5–9*	*10–14*	*15–17*	*All Ages*
Full-Time	34	42	39	52	39
Part-Time	26	30	38	19	29
Homemaker	37	22	18	19	28
Unemployed	4	6	6	10	5
Total	100	100	100	100	100
Number	N=226	N=122	N=85	N=42	N=475

EDUCATION OF THE PARENTS

There are benefits for children of having well-educated parents at home. This is particularly so for American Jews as Jewish women are more highly educated than other American women (Keysar and Kosmin 1995, 28). Figure 3.3 displays information on the educational attainment of Jewish parents. Among Jewish fathers, 35.6 percent had graduated high school (some of these attended college but did not graduate). Almost 29 percent graduated college with a B.A. or B.S. degree, over 14 percent went on to receive a master's degree, and 18.3 percent received a doctorate. For Jewish mothers, 41.9 percent graduated high school and did not attain a higher degree, and 29.2 percent graduated college with a B.A. or B.S. Over 17 percent went on to attain a master's degree and 6.8 percent acquired a doctorate.

High levels of education provide the foundation for the Jewish population's high socio-economic status. This human capital investment is one reason that 39 percent of Jewish men and 36 percent of Jewish women are in professional occupations, compared with only 16 percent of U.S. white men and women. Jews have historically placed great value on education. Today, particularly, well-educated people appreciate the importance and value of education for their children, and these high parental aspirations are expressed in the education they provide for them. Two sociologists, Cherlin and Celebuski (1982, 7), argue that Jewish parents encourage high educational attainment for their children by guiding them toward high-status occupations: "When asked what qualities they consider most desirable for children to have, contemporary Jewish parents were more likely than non-Jewish parents to stress qualities that reflect autonomy and self-direction; conversely, they placed a lower value on qualities associated with obedience and conformity to external authority. Thus, Jewish parents seem more likely to instill in their children those qualities that are congruent with the more

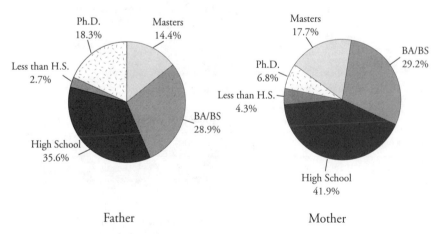

Father   Mother

Figure 3.3 Educational Attainment of the Parents of Core Jewish Children

highly rewarded and prestigious occupations in our society. In doing so, they probably enhance their children's chances of entering high-status occupations."

PRIVATE VERSUS PUBLIC SCHOOLING FOR CHILDREN

As their families' socio-economic status would suggest, a much higher proportion of
Jewish than other American children attend private schools: 38 percent versus 11 percent for American children overall. Nevertheless, parental decision making regarding
the type of schooling for their children can be quite complex. Choosing between a
private and a public school involves questions of desirability, availability and feasibility. Geography and finances play a role. The quality and academic reputation of the
public schools vary greatly by school district, and many parents pay a premium to pur-
chase a home in a neighborhood with a reputation for good schools. The availability
of private schools, either Jewish or of another type, also varies by place of residence.
Not every community provides Jewish day care or private Jewish school. Furthermore,
areas with Jewish schools may not provide a selection of schools of different Jewish
denominations or orientations. Those who live in rural areas or places with low Jewish population densities have even fewer possibilities. Of course, the choice within the
private sector of Jewish schooling, where it is accessible, reflects the value parents place
on Judaism following the prophetic dictum, "All your children shall be taught of the
Lord" (Isaiah). The economic feasibility depends on household income and the costs
that are involved in sending the children to any private school. Moreover, there are
parents who are strong believers in the public school system. Those who send their
children to public schools often provide a means for concurrently enhancing their
children's religious identity by sending them to afternoon Hebrew school or some
other supplementary program.

Table 3.7 shows that the type of school attended is correlated with household
composition. Children from single-parent households are only half as likely as children from two-parent families to enroll in private schooling, 21 percent versus 41 percent respectively. Thus, over 78 percent of the Jewish children who live with only one
parent receive public education, compared to only 59 percent of children who live
with two parents. This suggests that economic constraints might be the main consideration for single parents; the income of couple households is higher than for single-
parent households, so that more of them can afford to send their children to a more
expensive type of schooling.

Children who live with both parents are more likely to go to Jewish private
schools than children in any other household situation. Almost 41 percent of those
children receive private education, and this is split equally between Jewish schools and
other private schools. By contrast, only one-third of the children of single parents who
receive private education are enrolled in a Jewish program. It is possible that beyond
economic determinants other factors such as place of residence or the availability of
Jewish schooling are reasons why single-parent households are underrepresented in
Jewish day schools. Our data also show that in just over half of households that have
some children in a private Jewish school, parents earn over $60,000 a year, while about

Table 3.7 Type of Schooling of Core Jewish Children Age 5–17 by Household Composition

Household Composition	Schooling in Percentages				
	Public	Jewish-Private	Other Private	Total Percent	Total number
Couple, Couple + Others	59.5	20.4	20.1	100.0	691
Single Parent, Single Parent + Others	78.4	7.9	13.6	100.0	88
Total Number of Children*	62.1	19.0	19.0	100.0	796

*Includes children in non-normative households.

45 percent of those children in private secular education live in households with this high income. In contrast, only about 30 percent of households with children in public school earn over $60,000.

PATTERNS OF JEWISH EDUCATION OF THE CHILDREN

Jewish education is an essential ingredient of identity development and attainment; without Jewish knowledge, values, and beliefs, one may less likely be able to develop a meaningful Jewish identity. Furthermore, it is desirable that this acquisition occur in the early stages of life, so that it can make lasting impressions. Except in those homes that are both Jewishly traditional and where parents are able to properly convey an adequate amount of Jewish knowledge, the institution of formal Jewish education is extremely important in helping to ensure Jewish continuity. The level of Jewish education that Core Jewish children receive depends on four major factors: household structure, income, the age of the child, and the level of intensity of the household's connection to Judaism and Jewish institutions. Denominational status of the family (Orthodox, Conservative, Reform, etc.) and category of Jewishness (i.e., Jewish by Religion [JBR] as opposed to Jewish with No Religion [JNR]) reflect this association; less observant and more secularized families are much less likely to provide Jewish education for their children (Goldstein and Fishman 1993).

Household Structure and Jewish Education

Overall, just under half (46 percent) of the children aged 6–17 years have received any formal Jewish education (see Table 3.8). Children in two-parent families who live only with their parents or with their parents and other adults are more likely to have received Jewish education, 47 percent and 46 percent respectively, compared with only 32 percent among single-parent families. When other adults are present in single-par-

Table 3.8 Jewish Education of Core Jewish Children Age 6–17 by Household Composition

Household Composition	Percentage with some Jewish Education	Total Number of Children
Couple	47	805
Couple + Others	46	61
Single Parent	32	62
Single Parent + Others	44	39
Total*	46	989

*Includes children in non-normative households.

ent households, the likelihood of Jewish education rises to 44 percent. In this household type the extra adults are often grandparents, and the patterns may reflect their financial or moral influence. Though the sample size was only twenty-two cases, the proportion of children in non-normative families who receive Jewish education is about 41 percent.

As will be shown in later chapters, children living in homes with two married parents score better on a variety of socioeconomic measures, and are more likely overall to attain higher levels of Jewish practice and behavior. We will also see that for single-parent families, these measures tend to be higher when other adults are present in the household.

Age of the Child and Jewish Education

Figure 3.4 provides information on the number of Jewish children who had ever received a Jewish education by specific age categories. We can see that in ages 5–9, 174,000 or 48 percent of Jewish children had ever received a formal Jewish education. The proportion of children who had received a Jewish education is the highest in the 10–14 age group, the pre– and post–Bar/Bat mitzvah years; 163,000 or over 60 percent of Jewish children in that cohort have received some Jewish education. As there are larger numbers of Core Jewish children in the 5–9 age cohort than in the 10–14 age group, we project greater numbers of children receiving a Jewish education by the end of the decade.[9] Our data show that formal Jewish educational levels decline sharply after age 14. Moreover, in the formative years 5–9, the majority of Jewish children are not receiving any formal Jewish education. While affordability and economic conditions of the parents play a role, so does some parents' lack of interest in Jewish education as a priority.

Household Denomination and Jewish Education

In terms of denomination (see Table 3.9) Orthodox children are far more likely to have received a Jewish education; over 90 percent of children ages 6–17 have done so. About 60 percent of children in Conservative and 55 percent in Reform households

Age Group

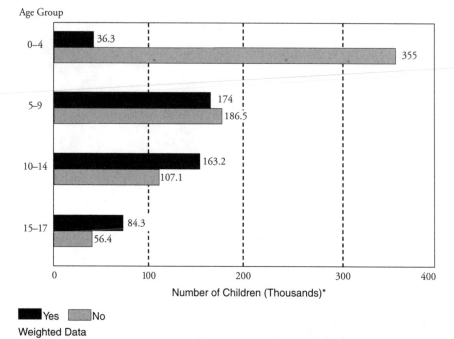

Yes No
Weighted Data
*Figures may not necessarily add to totals found in other places due to missing cases.

Figure 3.4 Core Jewish Child Population Ever Received Formal Jewish
Education

have received a formal Jewish education. Only about one in four children in families
with no specific denomination received any Jewish education.

If we compare children who are Jewish by Religion (JBR) to those who are Jewish with No Religion (JNR) we see that by age 17, 81 percent of the former had received some Jewish education but only 10 percent of the latter[10]. The type of Jewish

Table 3.9 Ever Received a Jewish Education by Denomination for Core
         Jewish Children Age 6–17

Denomination	Percentage
Orthodox N=63	92.1
Conservative N=222	60.4
Reform N=303	55.4
No Denomination N=72	23.6
Average N=660	57.1

schooling also correlates with the denomination of the household. In Orthodox homes, children usually attend full-time day schools or Yeshivoth. The concept of a day school is relatively new for Conservative and Reform Jews, and the majority who receive a Jewish education still participate in part-time programs such as afternoon Hebrew or Sunday school. The intensity and the scope of Jewish learning indeed vary tremendously by type of schooling. Jewish knowledge and skills which children acquire in day schools are greater compared to those acquired through limited supplementary Jewish education.

HOUSEHOLD COMPOSITION AND JEWISH CHARACTERISTICS OF THE FAMILY

Household Denomination and Family Type

The NJPS data enable us to link household composition to many Jewish characteristics of families with children. In comparing household denomination across the various types of household compositions for the total NJPS population (Table 3.10), Core and Non-Core, we find that regardless of religious orientation, about eight in ten households with children consist of a couple and children, i.e., conventionally structured nuclear families. For some groups the ratio of the conventional family reaches as high as nine in ten. Orthodox households, being the most traditional, are the most likely to contain children living only with their two parents and no other adult members.

Single-parent families occur most frequently in the No Denomination category—17.1 percent compared to only 4.7 percent among the Orthodox households.

Table 3.10 Household Composition of the Total NJPS: Percentage Distribution of the Child Population by Household Denomination

Denomination	Couple	Couple + Others	Single Parent + Others*	Total Percent**	Total Number
Orthodox	88.4	4.7	4.7	100.0	43
Conservative	80.2	5.2	13.4	100.0	172
Reform	79.2	7.7	11.3	100.0	221
No Denomination	73.0	8.1	17.1	100.0	111
Christian	80.5	8.0	10.3	100.0	87
Mixed Jewish/Non-Jewish	80.0	11.7	5.0	100.0	60
Other Religion	76.0	6.4	15.2	100.0	125
Total-All Denominations	78.8	7.2	12.2	100.0	819

*Due to small cell sizes, those households consisting of single parents living with no other adults and single parents living with other adult members have been combined.
**Also includes the small number of non-normative households.

Conservative and Reform fall between Orthodox and No Denomination with respect to percentage of couple households and single-parent families. Single-parenthood is also more frequent among those NJPS households with some Jewish background but currently Christian or another religion. The mixed households with a Jewish and non-Jewish adult have the highest proportion of couples who live with their children and others: relative or nonrelative members. This is to be expected, as some of these households include boarders, foreign-exchange students, household employees and other nonrelated individuals. We find non-normative families in all the denominations, but the small number of cases prevents us from making any valid conclusion. Comparative assessment of Table 3.10 shows that in most family-type categories, the Orthodox are somewhat set apart from the others.

Table 3.11 indicates the distribution of Core Jewish children by the denomination of the household. There are nearly 91,000 Jewish children being raised in Orthodox homes, 270,000 in Conservative homes, and almost 406,000 in Reform homes. The remaining 396,000 were being raised in households that were not self-identified with a Jewish denomination but instead mainly as Just Jewish, or in No Religion.

Synagogue Membership and Household Composition

Synagogue membership is another indicator of the Jewish character of the household and especially relevant for children because of its association with synagogue activities, e.g., Jewish education, Bar/Bat Mitzvah preparation, youth groups, and Jewish holiday celebrations. Comparing synagogue membership with household composition points to the Jewish environment and exposure of the children to Jewish culture and values. Since synagogue membership has an economic component as well as being a symbol of Jewish commitment, parental decisions with regard to the religious upbringing of their children must be analyzed, taking into account the economic status of the family.

Of the different family types, synagogue membership occurs most frequently among the two-parent constellation. The presence of children may trigger propensity

Table 3.11   Number of Core Jewish Children by the Jewish Denomination
of the Household (weighted data)

Denomination	Number of Children	Percentage of Children in the U.S. Jewish Population
Orthodox	90,700	7.8
Conservative	270,000	23.2
Reform	405,800	34.9
Other*	396,500	34.1
Total (N=1002)	1,163,000	100.0

*Includes other religion, miscellaneous Jewish, etc.

Table 3.12   Household Composition by Synagogue Membership for Households with
Core Jewish Children

	Syngagogue Membership		
Household Composition	*Percentage Yes*	*Total HHs %*	*Number*
Couple	51	100.0	451
Couple + Others	51	100.0	35
Single	34	100.0	41
Single + Others	44	100.0	23
Total*	49	100.0	563

*Includes the small number of non-normative households.

to join. Approximately 51 percent of these "nuclear families" are synagogue members. Single-parent families with or without other adults present in the household have the lowest rate of synagogue affiliation, only about one in three. As seen in earlier tables when other adults are present, the likelihood of membership increases (see Table 3.12).

The inclination of married couples with children to be synagogue members is exemplified in the fact that overall 49 percent of Core Jewish households with children belong to a synagogue, but among married Jewish couples age 18–45 with no children, only 26 percent belong to a synagogue. This large difference (23 percent) substantiates that some positive measures of Jewish connection are higher in households where children are present. Surely, Jewish education, as the usual prerequisite for Bar/Bat Mitzvah of the children, is a significant contributor to synagogue membership among families.

These tendencies are consistent with the conclusion of Friedman and Zober based on local community studies, "The pattern that seems to emerge indicates that so-called traditional families—those comprised of a married couple with children at home[11]—who identify with a particular stream of Judaism are more likely to be involved with a synagogue" (Friedman and Zober 1987, 20). Our data also show that over 90 percent of families with children who are currently receiving a Jewish education are synagogue members. Among households that have school-age children who are not receiving a Jewish education, fewer than 10 percent are synagogue members. These findings illustrate again the linkage between Jewish education and synagogue membership, emphasizing that families which choose to provide their children with formal and informal Jewish education are more likely to further expose them to the organized Jewish community by participating in synagogue activities.

As we can see from Table 3.13, the age of children in the household is associated with synagogue membership. Families with children ages 10–14 (around Bar/Bat Mitzvah time), are the most likely to be current synagogue members.

The age profile of synagogue membership for Core Jewish households with children reflects the pattern of the effectiveness of Jewish education. This pattern shows the direct impact of preparation for Bar/Bat Mitzvah. Sixty-two percent of Core Jew-

Table 3.13 Synagogue Membership for Core Jewish Households by Age of Children

Age of Child	Household Membership Percentage Yes Members	Total HHs %	Estimated number of children living in member households
0–4 N=320	39	100	152,000
5–9 N=309	54	100	194,000
10–14 N=247	62	100	167,000
15–17 N=141	58	100	81,000
Total N=1017	51	100	594,000

ish households with children in the 10–14 age cohort are members as compared to just 39 percent of households with children age 0–4. The falloff begins within a few years following the Bar/Bat Mitzvah ceremony: for households with children age 15–17, 58 percent belong (see Table 3.13). Overall, nearly 600,000 Core Jewish children live in households that belong to a synagogue. Lower fertility and older age at marriage, which was apparent in the period after the baby boom ended, impacted negatively on rates of synagogue membership. However, the current age structure and relatively large number of Jewish families with preteens suggests that the actual numbers of synagogue-affiliated households could rise by the end of the decade.

SUMMARY

Most Jewish children are raised in traditional nuclear families with two parents. Very few children have a large number of siblings since very few Jewish mothers have more than three children and most have less than three. Over 84 percent of Core Jewish children live in a household with two married adults, in most cases their biological parents. Just 13 percent of Jewish children live in single-parent households, far lower than the proportion of U.S. children overall who live in such households. For both the Jewish and general population, the proportion of single-parent households is higher than it was for earlier generations. Single parenthood is most frequent in households with older children. Single-parent households are overwhelmingly headed by females in both the Jewish and general populations, but male-headed single-parent households are slightly more common in the Jewish population. In cases of divorce and separation, female parents are more likely to attain custody in the U.S. population; however in the Jewish community male parent custody and shared custody arrangements are more common. There are nearly 160,000 Core Jewish children living in two-parent households consisting of a parent and stepparent. This represents 16 percent of all Jewish children living in two-parent households.

Most Jewish children are raised in relatively affluent households by well-educated parents. In general, children who live in two-parent households are more likely to live Jewishly than those in single-parent households. NJPS data reveal that the more Jewishly traditional the home, the more likely the child will associate with Jewish peers and join Jewish social activities. Thus, wealth and support from two-parent households have an impact on Jewish affiliation and connections. Parents in conventional nuclear families are much more likely to send their children to private schools and, in particular, Jewish schools and to be synagogue members. About two-thirds of mothers in conventional households work outside the home for pay while a slightly higher percentage of mothers in single-parent households do so. However, when other adults are present in these households, the mother is not as likely to work outside the home.

Approximately 400,000 Jewish children currently receive a formal Jewish education, of whom one-third are in Jewish day schools. Measures of Jewish identity are mutually reinforcing. For example, 90 percent of the families whose children receive Jewish education are also currently synagogue members. As would be expected, Orthodox Jewish children are more likely to receive a Jewish education and children raised in secular homes are the least likely. Orthodox children are also slightly more likely than those in other denominations to be living in two-parent households.

Jewish education and synagogue membership enhance a family's Jewish connections and involvement in the community. Our descriptive analysis illustrates the association between these Jewish connections and family structure, showing that children who are raised in traditional nuclear families are not only better-off socio-economically, but are also more Jewishly connected.

CHAPTER 4

PARENTAL DECISION MAKING REGARDING CHILDREN'S RELIGIOUS SOCIALIZATION

INTRODUCTION

There is both an ethnic and a religious dimension to being Jewish. From an ethnic perspective, NJPS showed that most people of Jewish descent choose to identify or define their offspring as Jews. In the religious sphere, however, matters are more complex, and parents exercise a wider range of options. In homogeneous Jewish families when parents are both Jews, the vast majority of children are raised within Judaism. Only 1.4 percent of families where both parents identify as Jews by Religion (JBR) raise their children without a religion. However, where both parents are Jewish with No Religion (JNR), none of the children are being raised in the Jewish religion: 58 percent are raised with no religion and 42 percent, some 19,000 children, in some religion other than Judaism, including New Age and Eastern religions. These latter children are not defined as part of the Core Jewish population. Furthermore, none of the couples in which both parents are secular Jews, even when they identify their children as Jews, provide them with any religious education. Thus, once again the "No Religion" category for ethnic Jews is a real commitment to secularism and a rejection of Judaism.

To better understand the complex reality of contemporary Jewishness as an ethnic-cultural-religious continuum, the NJPS adult respondents were asked about their identity as Jews, their current religion, and the religion into which they were born and raised. Children under age 18 were not interviewed, and the adult respondent in the household, usually one of their parents, classified their religious identity and upbringing according to their own criteria. Thus our data, both for adults and children, do not necessarily accord with halakhah (Jewish law) or denominational criteria regarding Jewish identity or affiliation. In short, these categories are self-defined sociological definitions rather than normative or legal ones.

In practice, parental decision is mostly confined to situations where there is a difference between the religious identities of the parents, and these decisions might be debatable. "A pluralistic society hypothetically allows couples relative freedom to choose the religion of their children. Everything else being equal, couples in religiously mixed households are as likely to choose one religion for their children as the other. However, everything else is not equal, and we will suggest that the pressures on intermarried couples appear to be toward raising their children in the dominant religion of the larger society or perhaps to take the path of least resistance and raise their children in a neutral, essentially agnostic manner" (Mott 1993, 3).

One of the earliest stories to emerge from the 1990 National Jewish Population Survey was that 52 percent of Jews by birth who married between 1985 and 1990, but only 9 percent of Jews who married prior to 1965, were in an interfaith marriage. This information, which triggered concern about the consequences of intermarriage, moved to the forefront of debate among the American Jewish public. In addition to the potential loss of people, there was also a fear on the institutional level about the community's future viability and continuity.

Previous reports and articles based upon the 1990 NJPS by Mayer (1993), and Mott and Abma (1993) have discussed such aspects of intermarried households as causality of mixed marriages, social service needs, religious concerns, and fertility. This analysis breaks new ground by comparing behaviors and Jewish practices of endogamous and interfaith families. A theoretical approach will be offered to parental decision making about the religious upbringing of their offspring. While these decisions are made on the family level, the consequences are felt on the community level, and help to determine the Jewishness of the next generation.

THE JEWISH CHILD POPULATION IN INTERFAITH FAMILIES—THE DATA

It is estimated that there are 2.64 million married persons who were born as Jews, and that 28 percent of these, 739,000, are currently married to non-Jews. Among these interfaith households there are 440,000 with a total of 664,000 children under 18. There are an additional 106,000 Jewish children being raised in households where a Gentile (either related or unrelated) other than the parent resides. Of the 1.9 million born Jews who married endogamously, 105,000, or 4 percent, are married to Jews by Choice (JBC). To fully understand the religious identities of these children would require in-depth interviews to ascertain how factors such as gender of the Jewish parent, divorce, remarriage, common-law relationships, age of the child, community of residence, and exposure to Jewish culture and religion affect the family.

Of all the household types identified in NJPS—people living alone, single parents, intermarried couples without children—the fastest growing household type is an intermarried couple with children. Moreover, because of the increased intermarriage rate, it is likely that within the next decade the majority of all children of Jewish parentage will have just one Jewish parent. Already, today there are a larger number of "Core" Jewish children under age 10 who live in interfaith families than live with only Jewish family members. This imbalance is greater, and thus more critical, in the youngest age group. Among children age 0–4, around 271,000 live in mixed families compared with 212,000 children in Jewish families. In older age cohorts we find more children in endogamous, or "all-Jewish," families.

Of the 664,000 children with both a Jewish and gentile parent, the majority are not raised in any religion, or are raised in a religion other than Judaism. These other religions may be syncretic forms of Judaism, Christianity, or something else.[12] As for children with a Gentile parent who were reported as being Jewish by their parents (either JNR or JBR), a slight majority of these 367,000 (200,000 + 167,000) Jewish chil-

Table 4.1 NJPS Child Population with a Core Jewish and Gentile Parent by Age

	Jewish Children with No Religion (JNR)		*Jewish Children by Religion (JBR)*		*Children with Other Religion (JCOR)*		*Total*	
Age	*N*	*%*	*N*	*%*	*N*	*%*	*N*	*%*
0–4	89,000	33.5	74,000	27.8	103,000	38.7	266,000	100
5–9	51,000	26.0	58,000	29.6	87,000	44.4	196,000	100
10–14	38,000	26.8	28,000	19.7	76,000	53.5	142,000	100
15–17	22,000	36.7	7,000	11.7	31,000	51.7	60,000	100
Total	200,000	30.1	167,000	25.2	297,000	44.7	664,000	100

dren are being raised with no religion. And the younger the age cohort, the higher the total number of Core Jewish children with a gentile parent. This reflects both the rising proportion of intermarriage and the high degree of secularization in these families.

Table 4.1 also indicates that while the number of children with a Core Jewish parent who are not being raised Jewish (JCOR) is highest in the 0–4 age cohort, their proportion is higher in the older age cohorts. Nearly 45 percent of the children in the sample who were defined as JCOR have a Core Jewish parent in their household.

The growing numbers and the rising proportion of children in interfaith families call for a detailed analysis of parental decision making in the religious socialization of these children. This would help predict identity outcomes on the aggregate level and identify points of intervention that could influence these outcomes.[13]

THEORETICAL FRAMEWORK

Since America may well be the most religiously identified of all modern societies, parents tend to expose children to some religious identity, as well as religious education, behavior, and practices in the home. Moreover, the separation of church and state that is so central to American life makes religion a personal, individual attribute. Family autonomy, then, is particularly strong in the religious realm and the influences of schooling and peer group, which supplement the socialization of children as they mature, are largely absent in the area of religious socialization. Despite this, the role of religion within the culture of the home has been ignored in the literature on child socialization.

We turn now to the consequences of parental differences in religious background on the way children are socialized.

Socialization of children, particularly as it relates to religion, is the by-product of collective decision making by the parents. Where the parents differ, the outcome of the decision-making process will follow basic principles of social exchange. Theorists (Safilios-Rothschild 1970; Rodman 1972; Scanzoni and Szinovacz 1980) have identified three key elements in the relative influence of spouses in family decision making: social resources, relative competence and interest, and culturally assigned authority by role. But this body of literature, too, ignores religion.

The social resources of the spouses include externally bestowed attributes such as education, professional status, power and prestige, assets and income. The relevance of these attributes to family decision making, however, varies by how much interest each spouse has in a particular family decision and how competent each believes he or she is to make the decision. Of course, every society bestows a certain amount of ascribed status to specific roles, particularly the role of parents, so that fathers and mothers operate with certain cultural assumptions about who is more or less qualified to make certain decisions about various aspects of children's socialization. In American society mothers are generally ascribed more authority over child socialization—"the hand that rocks the cradle"—particularly with regard to the psycho-emotional development of their children. This gives women leverage in determining their children's identity, including their religious identity. Nevertheless, this cultural advantage may be mitigated by the husband's greater social resources or his strong ideological or emotional commitment to his religion.

Contemporary research on the transmission of religious values from parents to adolescents (Dudley and Dudley 1986) supports the claim that mothers have greater influence on the value development of young people than fathers do. The values of mothers were found to be greater predictors of the values of the youth than those of the fathers among Seventh Day Adventist families. However, in families where parents are in disagreement on religious values, adolescents tend to agree with the less traditional parent, who is more likely to be the father.

THE THEORY IN ITS SOCIAL CONTEXT

Although most Americans have historically been highly endogamous—marrying within the same religious, ethnic, and social-class brackets—the past twenty years have seen a significant shift toward exogamy. The CUNY National Survey of Religious Identification found that in 1990 there were over 5 million Catholic-Protestant couples (Kosmin and Lachman 1993). Consequently, there is a growing population of children whose primary socialization experiences will be with parents who do not share a common religious and/or ethnic heritage. In interfaith families, parents are likely to differ in their religious interest and competence as well as in their cultural assumptions about their respective roles in imparting a religious identity to their children. This may lead to conflicts between spouses over the religious upbringing of the children.

Beyond religious differences, there is the obvious difference of gender, variations in educational, occupational and economic attainment, as well as differences in ethnic status that often characterize interfaith couples. The religious socialization of children is a negotiated parental decision unfolding within the context of all these other commonalities and differences.

This chapter, on intermarried households, examines the effects of each parent's gender, religiosity, and religious background on child-rearing decisions. It addresses the question of religio-cultural salience in intermarried households: which parent's religio-cultural heritage will dominate in the socialization of their children, and which socio-demographic characteristics of the parents can help predict dominance or compromise.

DATA

The analysis focuses on those 1990 NJPS households containing an intact marriage with children under age 18, in which the spouses reported differences in their current religious self-definition. Information was obtained for each member of the household in response to the question: "What is 'X's *current* religion?" with the response alternatives being

1. Jewish
2. Catholic
3. Protestant
4. Other
5. None

The response alternatives were reconfigured to create "Jewish," "Christian/ Other," and "None" types. Because the NJPS screening question ascertained which respondents were of Jewish parentage, it was possible to add a further refinement to the classification inasmuch as some respondents who acknowledged Jewish parentage nevertheless indicated that they currently profess no religion. Likewise, some respondents who indicated Christian or other non-Jewish parentage also replied that they currently profess no religion. On the basis of this scheme, couples were categorized by the type of difference between the spouses, and each was assigned a "religious difference score" (RDS) ranking the relative difference between them.

Depending on whether a couple differed in terms of their religious background and/or current religious self-definition, a numerical value was assigned estimating the degree of religious difference between them. Thus a couple in which both wife and husband were of Jewish background but only one of them currently professes being Jewish by religion was assigned a score of "1." At the other end of the spectrum, a couple in which one spouse was of Jewish background and currently professes being Jewish by religion and the other spouse currently professes being of the Christian faith was assigned a score of "5." Where one of the spouses currently professed being a Christian while the other spouse was of Jewish background but currently professed no religion, that couple was assigned a score of "4." Where one of the spouses was of Jewish parentage and currently professed the Jewish religion while the other spouse did not profess the Christian faith such a couple was assigned a score of "3." The score of "2" was assigned to couples in which one of the spouses was of Jewish parentage but now professed no religion and the other spouse was not currently of the Christian or any other faith.

The categories "JN" (Jewish/None) and "GN" (Gentile/None) refer to persons

Table 4.2 Current Religion of Spouses

Wife's Current Religion	Husband's Current Religion	RDS
Jewish (JR)	Jewish & None (JN)	1
Jewish (JR)	Christian/Other (CH)	5
Jewish (JR)	None (GN)	3
Jewish & None (JN)	Jewish (JR)	1
Jewish & None (JN)	Christian/Other (CH)	4
Jewish & None (JN)	None (GN)	2
Christian/Other (CH)	Jewish (JR)	5
Christian/Other (CH)	Jewish & None (JN)	4
None (GN)	Jewish (JR)	3
None (GN)	Jewish & None (JN)	2

whose origins were Jewish and non-Jewish respectively, but currently profess no religion. Thus, among respondents of Jewish origins, we distinguish between "Judaic" and "Jewish." The former profess Judaism as their religion; the latter profess no religion currently, but self-identify as Jewish, ethnically or culturally. Likewise, we distinguish between Christians and those professing some other religion, and persons who are of non-Jewish ancestry but currently profess no religion. We will call the latter "Gentiles" (GN). We excluded from the analysis those couples in which the spouses had identical current religious self-definitions. These scores, in combination with a series of other measures of spouse dissimilarity, are treated as the independent variables determining the religious socialization of children. Other items used to measure the spouses' social dissimilarity include

(a) American generational status (measured by the number of grandparents born in the United States);
(b) Educational attainment (measured by highest academic degree obtained);
(c) Occupational status (measured by occupational rank);
(d) Age gap between parents;
(e) Gender of Jewish parent.

Using the scores of the "Jewish-by-religion" parent on items (a) to (d), the relative social advantages of the two parents were ascertained. This created a measure of parental social dissimilarity in addition to their religious dissimilarity as established by the religious difference score (RDS).

Given the nature of the survey data, the research focuses on what choice parents make in responding to the question: What is the current religious identity of your children (measured here as a dichotomous variable: Jewish or Other/Christian/None)? The main research question is the probability of parents identifying their children as Jewish in a family where only one of the parents is Jewish. In the most general terms, it was hypothesized that the greater the total decisional leverage of the Jewish parent, the more likely that children will be identified as Jewish. The more equal the parents are in their decision-making power, the more equally their religious preferences will be represented in the socialization of their children, and therefore the less likely it is that they will identify their children as Jewish. The questions that remain are what favors the decisional influence of the Jewish parent over the non-Jewish parent, and by how much?

HYPOTHESES

It was postulated that in the America today:

(a) Mothers have more influence upon the religious identification of children than fathers;

(b) Parents who are themselves religiously identified have more influence upon the religious identity of their children than parents who are not themselves religiously identified;

(c) Jewish parents who have more personal knowledge of, or commitment to, their own Jewishness have greater influence upon the Jewish socialization of their children than those who have less knowledge or commitment;

(d) The decisional leverage of personal interest and cultural resources described in hypotheses (a), (b), and (c) will either increase or decrease when other social resources such as wealth and occupational prestige favor the Jewish or the non-Jewish parent.

The degree of dissimilarity between parents is causally linked to the decisions parents make about whether their children will be identified as Jewish. The total dissimilarity of couples will be a compound of their religious dissimilarity and the following additional components: the ethnic gap; the age gap; and the socio-economic gap (education and occupational rank). We believe that the direction of religious choice will be determined by the magnitude of religious difference between the parents and the relative social resources of the Jewish parent. Precisely in what proportions children are likely to be identified as Jewish in the various types of interfaith families is described below.

At this point, the analysis necessarily becomes fairly technical. To do justice to the data, to test the hypotheses, and to draw conclusions requires application of sophisticated statistical tools. Readers not interested in this level of technical detail may prefer to skip ahead to the section entitled "Beyond Religious Identity."

METHODOLOGY

First, we chose a model-free approach, the "Chi square Assisted Interaction Detection Method (CHAID)," to identify and analyze the complex relationships that may be embedded in higher-order contingency tables.[14]

Second, keeping in mind that CHAID is a multivariable procedure but not a multivariate one, this chapter also includes a logistic regression analysis, which explores the factors predicting parental decisions about the religious identification of their children.

The dependent variable in the logistic regression model is the religious identity of children: (1) Jewish; (0) Other/Christian/None.

The independent variables:

(a) Religious difference score of parents (RDS): (1) JR-JN; (2) JN-GN; (3) JR-GN; (4) JN-CH; (5) JR-CH;
(b) Which parent is Jewish: (1) mother; (0) father;
(c) Generational gap of parents: (1) The Jewish parent has more ancestors in the United States; (2) The parents have equal ancestry in the United States; (3) The Jewish parent has fewer ancestors in the United States;
(d) The Jewish parent has received Jewish education: (1) yes; (0) no;
(e) Secular education of the Jewish parent: (1) less than college; (2) college+;
(f) The gender of the child: (1) female; (0) male.

The logistic regression requires defining a reference group for each categorical variable. In our model, the last category, given in the above list of variables, was defined as the reference one.

FINDINGS

Before we present an analytical flowchart of the probability of children being identified as Jewish among the several independent variables, the table below summarizes the distribution of the outcomes of the dependent variable across the various categories of the main independent variable, described in Table 4.2, according to the religious composition of the parents.

As can be readily observed in Table 4.3, the highest probability of children being identified as Jewish occurs in those couples where one of the parents is Jewish by religion and the other is either Jewish without religion or a Gentile without religion. Both Jewish-by-religion mothers and fathers in an intermarriage are *most likely* to identify their children as Jewish if their spouse is a Gentile without religion and not involved in any religious group.

Mothers who are Jewish by religion are far more likely to identify their children as Jewish, even if they are married to a Christian spouse, than Jewish-by-religion fathers. Children are most likely to be identified as Christian in an interfaith marriage when their mothers identify themselves as Christian and the fathers are cultural, ethnic or secular Jews, i.e. Jewish without religion.

Table 4.3 suggests that different configurations of intermarriage are more or less likely to influence a Jewish identification for the children. But any expectation that such outcome is influenced in a straight-line manner by the degrees of difference in the religious identification of the parents (as described by the RDS categories outlined earlier) is not borne out by the data. A rank-ordering of the RDS categories shows

Table 4.3 Children's Religious Identity (Jewish, None, or Christian/Other)

Mother's/Father's Religious ID	Percentage Child's Religion Jewish		Percentage Child's Religion None	Percentage Child's Religion Christian/Other
JR/JN N=20	RDS=1	65	20	15
JR/CH N=103	RDS=5	58	20	22
JR/GN N=28	RDS=3	68	18	14
JN/JR N=25	RDS=1	56	28	16
JN/CH N=50	RDS=4	0	16	84
JN/GN N=12	RDS=2	8	75	17
CH/JR N=105	RDS=5	23	28	49
CH/JN N=69	RDS=4	7	30	63
GN/JR N=11	RDS=3	73	27	0
GN/JN N=14	RDS=2	0	100	0

that the highest likelihood of Jewishness being ascribed to children in intermarriages is in cases where RDS=1, 3, or 5, while the lowest likelihood is where RDS=2 or 4. Yet, these groupings or types of intermarriage would appear to be quite different from one another. Why are they associated with such similar probabilities for the present outcome variable? One possible explanation, suggested by the theoretical framework described earlier, is that other sources of influence available to each parent combine with the different RDS categories. It is this possible interaction that is explored in the section that follows.

The decision-making patterns of intermarried families are placed in perspective by the inclusion in our analysis of endogamous Jewish couples where both identify as Jews but one partner professes Judaism (JR) and the other does not (JN). In such cases around 60 percent of the children are raised in Judaism. When there is a Jew by religion (JR) intermarried with a Gentile of no religion (GN) the results are slightly more favorable for raising children in Judaism (around 70 percent). Furthermore, secular Jewish/Gentile couples (JN/GN) are almost invariably raising children without religion. These findings suggest that secular Jews are seriously opposed to raising their children in the Jewish religion. They also underline the declining importance of Jewish ethnic origin alone in transmitting Jewish culture across generations.

FLOWCHART ANALYSIS OF CHAID RESULTS

Figure 4.1 below is a graphic mapping of the apparent lines of interaction between the various categories of different independent variables and their relative likelihood of "producing" Jewish identification of children in intermarried families. As previously indicated, 31 percent of children in interfaith families are identified as Jewish.

While 42 percent of children of Jewish mothers are identified as Jewish, just 21 percent of those with Jewish fathers are. The study population of 456 children of interfaith families is split almost evenly between these two groups: 223 children have

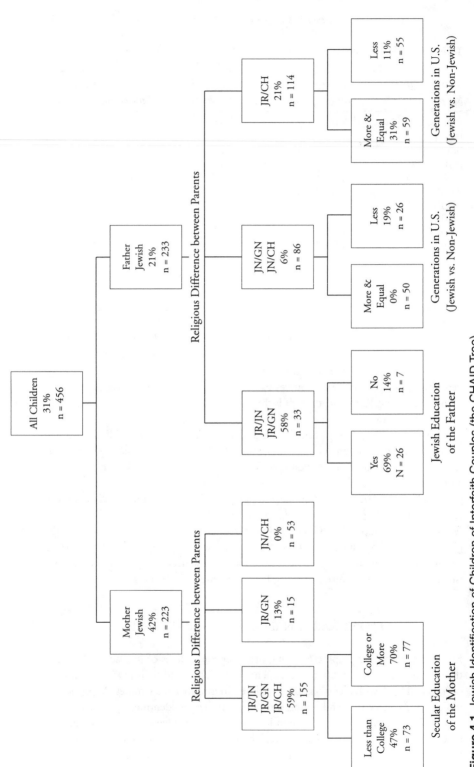

Figure 4.1 Jewish Identification of Children of Interfaith Couples (the CHAID Tree)

Jewish mothers and 233 children have Jewish fathers. In the next branch on the CHAID tree we focus on families where the mother is Jewish; the procedure chose RDS as the best predictor, merging three RDS categories into one group: JR/JN, JR/GN and JR/CH.[15] The second category consists of the JN/GN couples, and the third group consists of the JN/CH couples. When the mother is Jewish by religion, 59 percent of the children are identified as Jewish, compared with only 13 percent when the mother is Jewish with no religion and the father is Gentile with no religion. In the last category, JN/CH, none of the children is identified as a Jew. Continuing down to the next level, among Jewish mothers by religion the next best predictor is education of the Jewish partner—in this case, the mother. The higher the level of general education of the Jewish mother, the more likely that the children will be identified as Jewish (almost 70 percent among those with at least a college education). Among Jewish mothers with lower educational level (less than college) the next best predictor is the age of the children. More than half of children younger than 15 years old are likely to be identified as Jewish. None of the children in older age groups is identified as Jewish. (This branch is not shown in the chart.)

Looking further at the mother branch, we find no predictors within the significance level of 0.05 in those situations where Jewish mothers with no religion are married either to Gentiles with no religion (JN/GN) or to Christians (JN/CH).

Turning our attention now to the branch of the Jewish father, we find that the best predictor again is RDS. Yet the merged RDS categories are different from those of the Jewish mothers. The first category for Jewish fathers consists of JR/JN and JR/GN; the second, JN/GN and JN/CH; the third, JR/CH.[16] Thus, the main difference from Jewish mothers is the split within the Jews by religious subgroup, where those who are married to Christians stand as a separate group. While 58 percent of children of Jewish fathers by religion and secular mothers (Jewish or Gentile) are identified as Jews, only 21 percent of those who have Jewish fathers by religion and Christian mothers are identified as Jews.

The procedure detects the Jewish education of the respondent (not necessarily the father in the case of JR/JN couples) as the next best predictor in identifying Jewish children. Sixty-nine percent of parents who have ever received a Jewish education identify their children as Jewish, compared with only 14 percent among parents who have not received any Jewish education. Continuing down to the next level among Jewish fathers, we note that dissimilarity in the general educational level favoring the Jewish father increases the likelihood of children being identified as Jews to 100 percent, when one of the parents has received Jewish education.

Only 6 percent of secular Jewish fathers (of no religion) identify their children as Jews. But if the father's family has been in the United States for fewer generations than the family of the non-Jewish mother, the proportion of children identified as Jewish is 19 percent. At the other extreme, among couples where the Jewish father's family has been in the United States longer, all 50 children are identified as non-Jewish.

Interestingly, Americanization seems to have a quite different relationship in the case of men who are Jewish by religion married to Christian women (JR/CH). When the ancestors of the Jewish parent, in this case the father, have been in the United States for a longer time than those of the Gentile parent, then the children are almost three times more likely to be raised as Jews (31 percent) than when the Jewish parent has fewer generations in the United States (11 percent). One can only speculate as to why Americanness seems to be associated with less religious continuity for the children of non-religious Jewish men who intermarry, yet simultaneously associated with greater religious continuity for the children of men who are Jewish by religion and intermarry.

MULTIVARIATE ANALYSIS

Religious dissimilarity of parents is the most important factor predicting the religious identity of their children, according to the analysis of a stepwise logistic regression. The odds ratio for children being raised Jewish is the highest in families with Jewish-by-religion and Jewish-without-religion parents (JR/JN), or a Jewish-no-religion and a Gentile parent (JN/GN). Here we make a comparison to the reference category, families where one parent is Jewish without religion and the other is Christian (JN/CH).

The second notable factor in our model is the level of education of the Jewish spouse: college graduates are more likely to identify their children as Jews. The other vital factor influencing the religious identification of children is the immigrant generational gap between parents. When the Jewish parent has deeper roots in the United States, the likelihood of identifying the children as Jewish is higher than in families where the Jewish parent has fewer generations in the United States. These three variables are highly statistically significant, except for the category of the third variable where the parents have an equal number of generations in the United States (see Table 4.4). Surprisingly, the other variables in the model, namely gender of the child, Jewish education of parent, and even the gender of the Jewish parent, did not have a significant effect on the religious identification of children, once we looked at their effect while holding other factors constant in the multivariate analysis.

Table 4.4　Logistic Regression—Religious Identity of Children of Interfaith Families

Variable	Reference Category	B	Odds Ratio
Religious Difference	JN/CH		
JR/JN		3.233*	25.369
JN/GN		4.418*	82.924
JR/GN		2.885*	17.897
JR/CH		1.561*	4.762
Generational Gap	Jewish parent less time in U.S.		
Jewish parent: more		1.059**	2.883
Jewish parent: equal		−0.035	0.965
Educational Level of Jewish parent	College +		
less than college		−0.503*	0.605
Constant		1.388*	

*p< .001; **p< .005.

BEYOND RELIGIOUS IDENTITY

Specific religious behaviors of children are also of great interest to rabbis and communal leaders: Jewish education, holiday celebrations, philanthropy, religious practice, and associational patterns of children and their families. These are all paths in children's socialization that are associated with religious commitment. In the following descriptive comparison between endogamous and exogamous families, we learn more about Jewish children's ties and exposure to their heritage.

Jewish Education

Alice Goldstein and Sylvia Barack Fishman, in their report: "Teach Your Children When They Are Young: Contemporary Jewish Education in the United States," claim that, "Jewish education has an extended effect not only through its relation to the strength of Jewish identity of the individual who received the education, but through its impact on the kind and extent of Jewish education parents give their children" (Goldstein and Fishman 1993). This echoes an early tradition where it is claimed: "Educate the child in accordance with his way, and even in old age he will not depart from it" (Proverbs 22, 6). Therefore, the notion of an echo effect of Jewish education is very complex among interfaith couples and is relevant only for the Jewish partner. Goldstein and Fishman found that among children currently raised as non-Jews (yet living in households with Jewish adult[s]), only a few of those age 13 and above have ever received any Jewish education.

Comparing current endogamous and exogamous families in NJPS, we find that children with both Jewish parents are nearly six times more likely than children with only one Jewish parent to receive Jewish education (58.4 percent compared with 10.5 percent). In 1990 more than half of the children under age 18 lived in endogamous families (53.5 percent), and they are the consumers of the Jewish education programs. These programs are either less attractive to, or are not designed for, exogamous families, who are excluded in most cases by Jewish schools.

Since escalating intermarriage is a relatively recent phenomenon, the take-up of Jewish education by the age of the children warrants attention. Among the older age group, 10–17, Jewish education rates rise around the age of Bar/Bat mitzvah. There is, nevertheless, a large gap between children raised in endogamous and exogamous families. More than 80 percent of the children 10–17 in endogamous families, but just 16 percent in exogamous families, have received some Jewish education. In his report based on descriptive data, Lipset (1993) found that, in mixed marriages, a Jewish mother appears to be somewhat more important for Jewish educational continuity than a Jewish father, which could reflect the matrilineal nature of the Jewish religion.

Holiday Celebrations

Often referred to as "the December dilemma," the decision to celebrate Hanukkah, Christmas, both, or neither is complex and fraught with emotion. For many intermarried couples, the first occurrence in their marriage of the December holidays marks the beginning of a process of negotiation and compromise, and the course that is decided impacts all other religious and cultural issues.

Not surprisingly, nearly 90 percent of endogamous households with children light Hanukkah candles usually or all the time (see Table 4.5), as compared to only 53.4 percent of the interfaith households. At Christmas, the one non-Jewish observance that NJPS tested, less than 20 percent of endogamous family households have Christmas trees all the time but 90 percent of the interfaith households do so.

In observing four possible outcomes of celebrating these two December holidays—only Hanukkah, only Christmas, both holidays, or neither—we chose a subsample of NJPS families with children to learn about the Jewish or non-Jewish cultural milieu that the children in interfaith families experience.

The overwhelming majority of children in endogamous families—80 percent—celebrate only Hanukkah, and not Christmas at home. On the other hand, exogamous families celebrate either one festival or both. Twenty-eight percent celebrate only Christmas, and 62 percent celebrate both Hanukkah and Christmas. As expected, only a few families of either type do not celebrate either holiday. Among current endogamous families, there are a few who celebrate only Christmas. Examination of these families shows that some are remarriages, and were possibly exogamous in the previous marriage.

In addition to providing data on Christmas or Hanukkah practices in the two types of households, Table 4.5 gives further comparisons on holiday celebrations and practices of interfaith and endogamous households with children.

As would be expected, the other key measures of household identification with Jewish holidays are weaker in intermarried households than in endogamous households, and, in some ways, significantly so. For example, 85 percent of family households with two Jewish parents attend a Passover seder usually or all the time, as compared to only 44 percent of the interfaith family households. Similarly, for both Sabbath, and Purim, the endogamous households were significantly more observant. Only 16 percent of the interfaith households celebrated Purim in any way, but 60 percent of endogamous households did. The practice of not handling money on the Sabbath as well as the lighting of candles on Friday night were practiced to a much greater extent by endogamous households.

Giving Patterns

In terms of philanthropic behavior of adults, 70 percent of endogamous households gave to Jewish charitable causes, and 47 percent gave specifically to a Jewish federation or UJA campaign (see Table 4.6). For the interfaith households, the respective numbers were 29 percent and 14 percent. Needless to say, it is an issue of concern whether the current system of Jewish social services, which relies upon Jewish philanthropic giving, can maintain itself if the intermarriage rate keeps rising and current giving patterns persist.

Table 4.5 Holiday Celebrations and Practices in Interfaith and Endogamous Households
with Children (in percentages) (N = 566)

Observance or Practice	N=249 1 Parent Jewish	N=317 2 Parents Jewish
Attend Passover Seder (usually or all the time)	44.1	85.4
Never have an Xmas Tree	10.0	81.4
Light Hanukkah Candles (usually or all the time)	53.4	89.5
Attend Purim Celebration	16.1	60.3
Light Sabbath Candles (usually or all the time)	3.2	37.2

Table 4.6 Jewish Charitable Giving in Interfaith and Endogamous
Households with Children (in percentages) (N = 566)

Giving Category	N=249 1 Parent Jewish	N=317 2 Parents Jewish
Contribute to a Jewish Charity	28.9	70.3
Contribute to UJA/Federation	13.7	46.7

Participation in Jewish Activities

The participation rates in Jewish communal activities are also comparatively very low
for interfaith families (see Table 4.7). Just 16 percent belong to a synagogue, as compared to two-thirds of the endogamous households. Just 10 percent of interfaith children receive a Jewish education, while over half of the children who have two Jewish
parents do.

Jewish social and recreational activities enroll few children from interfaith
households. Only 4 percent of these families belong to a Jewish community center,
just 7 percent of the children attend Jewish camps, and a mere 2 percent of the chil-

Table 4.7 Membership/Participation in Interfaith and Endogamous
Households with Children (in percentages)

Activity	1 Parent Jewish	2 Parents Jewish
Current Synagogue Members N=566	16.1	65.6
Current JCC Membership N=178	3.6	32.6
Children received a Jewish Education N=1030	10.5	58.4
Children went to a Jewish Camp N=1030	7.0	20.8
Children in Jewish Youth Group N=1030	2.1	16.1

Table 4.8   Attributes of Interfaith and Endogamous Households with Children
(in percentages) (N = 566)

Attribute	N=249 *1 Parent Jewish*	N=317 *2 Parents Jewish*
Closest Friends Jewish (all or most)	10.8	54.7
Jewish Character of Neighborhood (very or somewhat Jewish)	18.1	46.4

dren belong to a Jewish youth group. For the children in endogamous households, the figures are much higher, 33 percent, 21 percent, and 16 percent respectively.

Social Networks

Finally, family social networks are markedly different in the two family types: 55 percent of endogamous parents report that or all or most of their closest friends are Jewish, and 46 percent report living in a neighborhood that is very or somewhat Jewish (see Table 4.8). For the children of interfaith couples, these aspects of a Jewish social environment are largely absent, only 11 percent and 18 percent respectively.

SUMMARY

Many Jews are making decisions for their children that do not bode well for Judaism. Secular Jews continue their alienation from the Jewish religion into the second generation, while among interfaith families, less than one in three children is raised as a Jew. Interfaith couples with children constitute the fastest-growing household type in the Jewish community, and this is especially true for households with children under the age of 5. As less than a third of the children of exogamous marriages are being raised in the Jewish religion, we need to investigate the roles that Judaism and socialization play in the culture of the home.

Multivariate analysis uncovered the fact that children in interfaith households are most likely to be raised Jewish when the Gentile spouse does not practice any religion. Level of education of the Jewish parent is an important factor too, since college graduates are more likely to raise their children as Jews. Another factor in the positive Jewish identification of the children is how deep the American roots of the Jewish parent are. The anticipated special significance of mothers in the religious upbringing of children, detected in the CHAID analysis, disappears once controls are introduced in the multivariate analysis.

Finally, a variety of other Jewish religious and social activities were examined such as celebrating Hanukkah, attending a Passover seder, observing the Sabbath, giving to Jewish charity, belonging to a synagogue, and belonging to a JCC. In each case, members of endogamous households were much more likely to observe, practice, or participate in the Jewish activity or ritual. For child-centered activities—attending Purim carnivals, going to a Jewish camp, belonging to a Jewish group, etc.—the pattern was the same. Associational measures such as a tendency to live in a Jewish neighborhood or to have mostly Jewish friends produced similar results. In sum, for this population the religious identity the parents choose for their children, whether Jewish, secular, or another religion, is directly translated into social reality and behavior. There is a clear consistency between the parents' description of their children's religious identity and the religious socialization they provide for them in terms of religious education, home practices, and community involvement.

What are the long-term consequences of decisions by parents in interfaith families about their children's religious socialization? Social learning theory asserts that children may imitate and identify with a particular parent (Openshaw, Thomas, and Rollins 1983). Following this assertion, in families where more than one religious model is available, children will imitate the more dominant and powerful one. Our findings suggest that this will not necessarily be the Jewish parent. In other interfaith families, children will not identify exclusively with either parent, and will consequently live with religious ambiguity. From the Jewish community's perspective, the long-term consequences are not favorable in either case.

CHAPTER 5

LIVING IN A UNIQUE
JEWISH ENVIRONMENT:
THE CHILDREN OF NEW YORK

INTRODUCTION

Jewish New York

Louis Wirth claimed: "If you want to know what kind of Jew a man is, ask him where he lives; for no simple factor indicates as much of the character of the Jew as the area in which he lives. It is an index not only to his economic status, but also to his religion and his outlook on life and the stage in the assimilative process that he has reached" (1928, 283).

New York City, the largest city in the United States, also has the largest urban Jewish population, not only in the United States but in the world. In 1991, the Jewry of Greater New York—including New York City, Nassau, Suffolk, Westchester, and Rockland counties—was estimated at 1.5 million, or 16 percent of the total population, according to Bethamie Horowitz (1993). The unique setting of Greater New York and the sheer size of its Jewish population provide an exceptional variety of religious, social, and cultural Jewish life. In New York City, Jews are not simply one minority among others. Because of the size of the Jewish community, internal differences are finely defined, and Jews distinguish themselves from other Jews on ideological or religious grounds. Nonetheless, Jews in New York City can find enough other Jews similar to themselves to fill an apartment building, an organization, or even a neighborhood (Moore 1994, 5). The full denominational spectrum of American Judaism is represented in New York. There are not only synagogues of the Orthodox, Conservative, Reform, and Reconstructionist branches, but also houses of worship that are not connected to any of these primary movements.

No other community outside Israel can claim the high level of Jewish intensity that New York City and its surroundings manifest. According to *The 1991 New York Jewish Population Study* (Horowitz 1993), the city, which comprises the five boroughs—Manhattan, Brooklyn, the Bronx, Queens, and Staten Island—is home to 1,027,000 Jews. The suburban counties in New York State which are also included have an additional 476,000 Jews. Jewish households are especially concentrated in particular areas. Neighborhoods that are more than 30 percent Jewish include Riverdale in the Bronx, Midwood, Borough Park, Canarsie, Sheepshead Bay, and Manhattan

Beach in Brooklyn, Lower Midtown and Murray Hill in Manhattan, and Forest Hills, Rego Park, and Fresh Meadows in Queens. The Five Towns and Great Neck areas of Nassau County on Long Island, as well as Scarsdale in Westchester County and Spring Valley and Monsey in Rockland County, are also more than 30 percent Jewish. In addition, New York remains a magnet for Jews from other countries seeking a better life—many of the most recent immigrants are secular Russian Jews.

Orthodoxy, the smallest branch of American Jewry, is noticeable and influential in the New York area. While the estimated Orthodox population nationwide, including New York, is about 7 percent of the Jewish population, in Greater New York Orthodox Jews are about 14 percent of the Jewish population. Greater New York also has a higher proportion of Jews with an Orthodox upbringing than Jews in the rest of the country—26 percent and 15 percent respectively. Moreover, the proportion of Orthodox Jews who maintain their denominational upbringing is far higher in New York, 44 percent compared with 15 percent outside New York. This phenomenon strengthens the traditional religious ambience of New York. The Orthodox community's political and economic power is well recognized in New York by both Jews and non-Jews. Thus the Orthodox community's contribution to the religious and cultural atmosphere of New York goes beyond its relatively small numbers. The relatively large and visible Orthodox community establishes an atmosphere of religious expression that possibly also comforts or reassures some secular Jews. There are many Orthodox neighborhoods, such as Borough Park, Crown Heights, Williamsburg, and Monsey. In fact, there are more Orthodox synagogues than any other type in the region, particularly in New York City.

Jewish life in the New York area provides a wealth of religious services, social programs, and cultural activities. The number of Jewish organizations is enormous, including synagogues, community centers, YM-YWHAs, museums, institutions of higher learning (for example, Yeshiva University, the Jewish Theological Seminary, and Hebrew Union College), Jewish day schools, Jewish day-care centers, Jewish nursing homes, and numerous others.

Jewish educational opportunities in New York are greatly enhanced by the devotion of entire sections of public libraries and general bookstores to Jewish themes. Jewish community centers fill a need for recreational activity, social programs, cultural events, camping, and other activities, especially for youth. New York also offers a tremendous variety of Jewish ethnic cuisine and Kosher restaurants.

All these institutions and organizations create a special Jewish lifestyle and culture in New York. Although they affect the whole family, many are geared primarily towards children. The easy access to a Jewish school, a Yeshiva, a Jewish community center, or a Jewish restaurant makes Jewish lifestyle easy to maintain. As Dash-Moore describes it, "Being Jewish came naturally in New York; it required virtually no special effort. It was part of being a New Yorker, or to be more precise, of being from Brooklyn or the Bronx" (Dash-Moore 1994, 6).

New York has always offered vast economic opportunities. The occupational composition of New York Jews has shifted since the last large wave of new Jewish immigrants in the late-nineteenth and early-twentieth century. New York Jews have moved from light manufacturing—the garment industry, for example—to other oc-cupations in the professions and service industries. Furthermore, the special Jewish environment has significant effects on Jewish children's experiences. This chapter fo-cuses on different aspects of New York children's lives, such as education, religious celebrations, social activity, and household structure, in comparison to Jewish chil-dren in other regions of the country.

Research Questions and Data

The unique social and urban environment of New York raises many research ques-tions:

(a) What religious and social Jewish expressions are children in New York ex-posed to? In what ways are these different from those affecting children re-siding outside of New York?
(b) How does the parents' background influence the religious upbringing of their children? Do parents in New York differ from their counterparts na-tionwide in this respect?
(c) Do the more affiliated Jews in New York have children who are more in-volved in the Jewish community? Do the children of interfaith families fol-low the same pattern as children with endogamous parents?
(d) Does just living in a more intense Jewish environment substitute for for-mal affiliation in its effect on Jewish identity?

The comparison between New York Jewish children and those residing outside the Greater New York area is based on both *The 1991 New York Jewish Population Survey* (NYJPS) and *The 1990 National Jewish Population Survey* (NJPS). The NYJPS is a random representative sample of 4,512 Jewish households that were identified through a screening and interviewing process similar to that of NJPS. Both studies also used ICR Survey Research Group of Media, Pennsylvania, to conduct the sam-pling and interviewing. More than 35,000 residents of New York City and Nassau, Suffolk, Westchester, and Rockland counties were contacted by telephone to locate and qualify Jewish households, that is, households containing at least one person who is currently Jewish or was Jewish in the past. The screening and interviewing phase began in November 1990 and was completed in May 1991 (Horowitz and Solomon 1992).

Throughout this chapter, data that refers to New York was obtained from NYJPS, while data on national Jewish population was obtained from NJPS. The com-parisons between NYJPS and NJPS are possible and meaningful due to their similar questionnaires. In most cases the same questions were asked in both studies. To allow statistical inferences about the significance of the differences found in the analyses, a special data set was created which combines the two samples. The comparisons will be presented in two forms—first descriptive and then analytic.

THE DEMOGRAPHIC CHARACTERISTICS
OF THE CHILDREN OF NEW YORK

Age and Gender

The age composition of New York Jewish children is similar to that of the national sample (see chapter 2, Table 2.1). About a third of the 377,000 children under the age of 18 living in Jewish households in the Greater New York area are under age 5, quite similar to the 32 percent nationally. An additional 29 percent are in the 5–9 group compared to 31 percent nationally (see Table 5.1). Just over 100,000 children are in the 10–14 age group, comprising slightly more than a quarter of the Jewish children living in New York. The smallest group is age 15–17, which includes only about 12 percent of the Jewish children, similar to the national percentage. In general, children under age 18 are 25 percent of the Jewish population in Greater New York, again similar to the share of children in the Jewish population nationally (23 percent).

The ratio of males to females under age 18 is 110, similar to the ratio of 109 found in the national survey for the Core Jewish child population. The ratio of males to females exceeds 110 in children ages 5–9 and 15–17.

THE RELIGIOUS AND SOCIAL
JEWISH ENVIRONMENT OF CHILDREN OF
NEW YORK AND THE UNITED STATES

We seek to determine the effect of New York's unique social and cultural Jewish environment. In this section Jewish households with children in Greater New York (the nine counties) are compared with the national Jewish population excluding the nine counties on the variables of Jewish education, synagogue membership, Hanukkah and Christmas celebrations, and contributions to charities.

Table 5.1 Number and Percentage Distribution of Children Living in Jewish Households in Greater New York by Age and Gender

Age	Male	Female	Total	% of 0–17
0–4	58,538	59,172	117,710	31.3
5–9	62,995	46,993	109,988	29.2
10–14	49,530	51,168	100,698	26.7
15–17	26,132	22,071	48,202	12.8
Total	197,195	179,404	376,599	100.0

Source: 1991 NYJPS.

Weighted data.

Table 5.2 Percentage Distribution of Children Living in Households with at Least One Core Jewish Parent in Greater New York by Age and Religion Raised

	Religion Raised					
Age	Jewish	Catholic	Protest.	Other*	None	Total
0–4	88.8	2.9	0.5	0.6	7.2	102,961
5–9	88.9	4.1	0.4	1.2	5.3	97,059
10–14	90.7	4.2	0.2	0.8	4.1	94,213
15–17	89.9	2.1	2.0	1.6	4.3	44,526
Total	89.5	3.5	0.6	1.0	5.4	338,758

Weighted data from 1991 NYJPS.
*Other religions.

Children by Age and Religious Upbringing

As Table 5.2 shows, a strong majority, nearly 90 percent, of the children who live in families with at least one Core Jewish parent in New York are raised as Jewish; only 5.1 percent of the children are raised in other religions, and 5.4 percent are raised with no religion. The distribution of the religions in which children are raised varies only slightly by age. Among youngest children (the age group 0–4) more are in the no religion category, 7.2 percent, as compared to 4.1 percent among those aged 10–14. It is assumed that children who are raised in any religion other than Judaism are the product of interfaith families, either from current or previous mixed marriages.

Children's Participation in Jewish Social Activities

Various opportunities exist for children in the United States and in Greater New York to participate in informal Jewish educational activities in leisure hours and vacation time. For purpose of comparison, the participation of Jewish children (at least one of whose parents is a Core Jew) in Jewish camps (day and overnight) and youth groups is examined. Jewish values and tradition are learned by young people, and Jewish rituals are practiced—to different degrees—in these institutions. A variable was constructed that divides the children into four categories: those who participated in both types of activity in the past year, those who only attended a Jewish camp, those who participated only in a Jewish youth group, and those who participated in neither. Our goal is to compare children's activities in and outside New York.

Figures 5.1 and 5.2 show similar patterns in the national and the New York Jewish communities, but the intensity of involvement is quite different. Children in and outside New York tend to be more active in Jewish camp or youth group in their teenage years than before. This pattern contrasts with the falloff in formal Jewish education after age 13. Nevertheless, children residing in New York generally participate

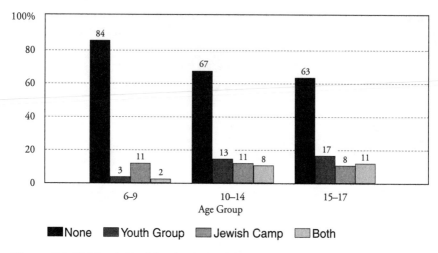

Figure 5.1 Children's Participation in Jewish Activities in the U.S (excluding greater N.Y.)

more in these activities than children outside of New York. Proportionally fewer children in New York are in the large "none" category, that is, don't participate in any activity. For instance, in the 10–14 age group only 50 percent in New York are in the "none" category, compared to 67 percent outside New York.

Looking at the minority of children who did go to a Jewish camp, the gaps between the two Jewish environments are quite substantial for all age groups. In New York, 21 percent of children 10–14 and 16 percent of those 15–17 went to Jewish

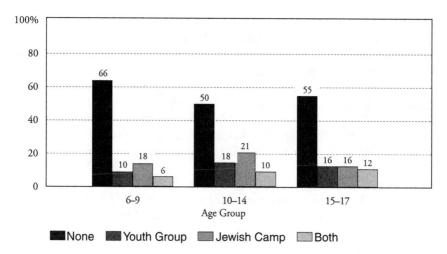

Figure 5.2 Children's Participation in Jewish Activities in Greater New York

summer camp in 1989–1990, compared with only half that proportion outside of New York: 11 percent and 8 percent respectively. Clearly children in New York have more opportunities to participate in these informal Jewish educational activities and have more options to choose from. Yet, participation depends not only on availability but also on the desire to participate. It remains a research question whether the desire to participate in Jewish youth groups or summer camps is different in and outside New York.

Children of Interfaith Families

Interfaith families are less prevalent in New York than outside for all Jewish denominations. Thirty-four percent of first marriages occurring between 1985 and 1990 among Conservative Jews in New York and 39 percent among Reform Jews were mixed marriages. For those residing outside the New York area, mixed marriages during that same time period comprised 55 percent of first marriages for those raised Conservative, and 64 percent for those raised Reform. The Orthodox respondents in New York exhibit very low rates of intermarriage. Over 93 percent of those who had an Orthodox upbringing and married between 1985–1990 had a Jewish spouse. In the national sample, the small subsample of Orthodox prevents us from describing their recent marriage patterns.

How different are children of interfaith families raised in New York from those raised elsewhere? Overall, 22 percent of Jewish children in New York live in interfaith families, compared with 48 percent outside New York. The proportion raised in the no-religion category among interfaith families is similar in both populations. However, 42 percent of the New York children in such families are raised in Judaism, as compared with only 23 percent of their counterparts outside New York. Following Table 5.3, we find that even among endogamous families, fewer children are raised in the Jewish religion outside New York.

Not only is the proportion of children living with a Gentile parent less than half in New York than elsewhere, but children in exogamous households are almost twice as likely to be raised Judaically in New York.

Table 5.3 Children of Interfaith Families by Religion Raised New York and Nationwide

	Percentage NATIONAL (excluding N.Y.)		Percentage NEW YORK	
Religion Raised	*Endogamous Family*	*Exogamous Family*	*Endogamous Family*	*Exogamous Family*
Jewish	89	23	99	42
Other	4	54	0.2	38
None	7	23	0.8	20
Total Percent	100	100	100	100
Total Number	447	417	1865	517

Parents' Background and the Religious Upbringing of Children

Synagogue Membership

Synagogue members tend to participate in many Jewish religious and social events. Their children are more likely to receive Jewish education under the auspices of the synagogue, to have a Bar/Bat Mitzvah, and to be more involved in Sabbath worship and holiday services with their families.

Jewish families (containing a Core Jewish parent) with children in the New York area are more likely to be synagogue members than similar families outside the area by a margin of 14 percent (54 versus 40 percent, see Table 5.4). We can assume that children who reside in the New York area are more exposed to synagogue activities, both religious and social, than their counterparts nationwide. One explanation for the difference in rates of synagogue membership is the large Orthodox community in New York. In the later multivariate analysis, we can assess to what degree denominational background correlates with synagogue membership. Another explanation, of course, might be the relatively large number of synagogues in New York.

Jewish Education: Two Generations—Parents and Children

Is there a difference between New York and the rest of the country in how parental background influences the religious upbringing of children? The first aspect explored is Jewish education. Goldstein and Fishman indicate that the "number of years of parents' education is very clearly reflected in the number of years of education being given their children. Where both parents have had no Jewish education, almost two-thirds of the children have also received no such schooling. By contrast, if both parents had six or more years of Jewish school, some nine out of ten of their children have as well" (1993, 17).

Both fathers and mothers in New York who had themselves received Jewish education are more likely than their counterparts outside New York to expose their children to Jewish education (see Table 5.5). The relative difference is larger among fathers than mothers. Overall, the mother tends to be the parent to pass the torch of

Table 5.4 Synagogue Membership of Households with Children Containing
              a Core Jewish Parent

Synagogue Membership	National (excluding N.Y.)	New York
Yes	40	54
No	60	46
Total Percent	100	100
Total Number	477	1,391

Chi-Square=27.9; significance=.0001.

Table 5.5 Jewish Education of Core Jewish Parents and Children New York and Nationwide

| | *Jewish Education of Children* | | | |
| | *Children Nationally (excluding N.Y.)* *N=544* | | *Children in New York* *N=1673* | |
Jewish Education-Parents*	*Percent of Children Receiving Jewish Education*	*Total*	*Percent of Children Receiving Jewish Education*	*Total*
Father yes	50	100	76	100
Father no	20	100	46	100
Mother yes	67	100	84	100
Mother no	36	100	65	100
Overall Yes	59	100	80	100

*This refers to the respondent.

Jewish learning to the next generation. In New York, 84 percent of the mothers who received Jewish education raise children who also receive Jewish education, compared with 76 percent of the fathers. Outside New York, 67 percent of the children whose mothers had Jewish education themselves get a Jewish education, compared with 50 percent of those whose fathers had Jewish education.[17]

Three-quarters of Jewish children age 6–17 who reside in New York receive Jewish education, while only half of those outside the New York area do.[18] While one can argue that the large New York Orthodox community contributes to this gap, a more complicated question is raised: Are New Yorkers exposing their children to Jewish education because they are more committed to a Jewish way of life, or is it simply a consequence of greater availability and access? Further, is the poor quality of public schools, whether real or perceived, in New York and other urban centers, motivating parents to send their children to private Jewish schools?

Holiday Celebrations

Celebrations of Jewish and/or Christian holidays are important indicators of the Jewish identity of households (Goldstein 1992, 133–137) and thus, of children's exposure to and participation in Jewish rituals. To examine the practice of Jewish and Christian rituals among families with children a new variable was constructed that includes the celebration of Hanukkah and Christmas.

As the figures in Table 5.6 indicate, an overwhelming majority (76 percent) of the families in New York celebrate only Hanukkah and not Christmas, as compared with only 45 percent of the families in the rest of the nation. Furthermore, 34 percent of the Core Jews outside New York celebrate both Hanukkah and Christmas, while just 19 percent of the Core Jews in New York do so. Another way to illustrate

Table 5.6 Hanukkah and Christmas Celebrations in the Households Containing Core Jews

Hanukkah/Christmas	National (excluding N.Y.)	New York
Neither	3	1
Only Christmas	18	4
Both	34	19
Only Hanukkah	45	76
Total Percent	100	100
Total Number	477	1393

Chi-Square=174.4; significance=.0001.

how New York Jewry preserves Jewish rituals is to look at those families who celebrate only Christmas. A substantial percentage of Core families in the rest of the nation, 18 percent, do so while not celebrating Hanukkah at all. Many of these are probably interfaith families where one of the parents is a practicing Christian. In New York, though, just 4 percent of Core Jewish families only celebrate Christmas.

Analysis of Variance

We previously raised the question of whether residing in New York enhances synagogue membership and exposure of children to Jewish education, holding other cultural and demographic variables constant. A multivariate analysis was employed to assess the likelihood of household's current synagogue membership. Analysis of variance of synagogue membership among households with children (Table 5.7) aims to explicate the question of the contextual effects of residing in New York. Included in the model are variables that were found to be important in the descriptive analysis, such as Jewish denomination and endogamy versus exogamy. Additionally, household income was held constant since synagogue membership raises financial considerations in addition to religious and social ones. Age of the oldest child is another important variable added to the model, since families are more likely to join synagogues as children approach the age of Bar/Bat Mitzvah. Readers who are not interested in technical details should skip ahead to the summary.

Findings

The analysis of variance indicates that all the independent variables except place of residence are statistically significant at the .001 level. No other two-way interactions between the independent variables in the model except that between intermarriage and Jewish denomination were found. Thus we can assume an additive model and look at the results of the multiple classification analysis. Parenthetically, it should be noted that the analysis of variance is used rather than logistic regression (given that the dependent variable is dichotomous) since the distribution of the dependent variable is in the range of 40–60 percent. In this range the results of both forms of analysis are virtually the same.

Table 5.7 provides a Multiple Classification Analysis. For synagogue membership, the most important explanatory factor was found to be the combined variable: intermarriage/ denomination. Endogamous families (both parents are Jewish) that are Orthodox or Conservative are by far more likely to be synagogue members: 90 percent of Orthodox and 68 percent of Conservative endogamous families were found to be synagogue members. The grand mean in the model is 0.51, and the endogamous Reform families reflect the average household with 51 percent synagogue membership. Interfaith families are rather homogeneous, regardless of the denomination of the Jewish parent; they are far below the grand mean with only 20 percent having synagogue memberships.[19] Exogamous secular families have the lowest membership rate, below 10 percent.

Both demographic variables, household income and age of the oldest child, are significant and add to our model. As expected, families with low income levels are the least likely to join a synagogue while those with high income are the most likely to do so. The relationship between synagogue membership and income is linear, i.e., the higher the household income, the higher is the likelihood of a synagogue member-

Table 5.7 Multiple Classification Analysis of Synagogue Membership

Variable/category Grand Mean=.51	Effect	N
1. Intermarriage/Denomination	beta=.52	
Endogamous/Orthodox	.39	222
Endogamous/Conservative	.17	307
Endogamous/Reform	0.00	368
Endogamous/secular	−.20	53
Exogamous/Conservative+Orthodox	−.34	85
Exogamous/Reform	−.31	197
Exogamous/secular	−.43	89
2. Place of Residence	beta=.04	
National (excluding N.Y.)	.04	325
Greater New York	−.01	996
3. Household Income	beta=.17	
less than 20K	−.18	68
20K–39K	−.11	223
40K–59K	−.03	333
60K–79K	.01	247
80K–124K	.08	262
125K and over	.12	188
4. Age of Oldest Child	beta=.15	
0–4	−.11	355
5–9	−.02	350
10–14	.09	338
15–17	.06	278
Multiple R Squared = .328		

ship, and vice versa. Only a third of the families with household income of less than $20,000 are synagogue members, compared with 63 percent of those with an annual income of $125,000 and over. Thus synagogue membership is closely related to economic means, independent of other variables such as religious denomination.

As the oldest child approaches Bar/Bat Mitzvah, the likelihood of synagogue membership of the family increases. Families where the oldest child is preschool (0–4 years old) are the least likely to join a synagogue, only 40 percent of them doing so, while those with children ages 10–14 are the most likely to be synagogue members (60 percent). Overall, the model explains 33 percent of the variance in synagogue membership.

The most interesting finding is that living in New York has no independent effect. Once Jewish religious and demographic variables, such as denomination and type of marriage, as well as income and age of the oldest child are held constant, the differences between residing in or outside of New York in synagogue membership disappear.

Jewish Education of the Focal Child[20]

Since the above finding on differentials between New York and the national population in synagogue membership was unexpected, it calls for further analysis using another variable, Jewish education. Table 5.8 provides a Multiple Classification Analysis of the current Jewish education of the focal child. The analysis of variance once again indicates that place of residence is not statistically significant in explaining children's Jewish education, while other independent variables are statistically significant. Intermarriage/Jewish denomination and the age of the focal child are significant at the .001 level, and Jewish education of the parent at the .05 level. Overall, the two-way interactions effect is statistically insignificant, though we can detect some interaction between the combined variable intermarriage/denomination and the age of the focal child. Nevertheless, we can still assume an additive model. The grand mean in this model is .46, that is, almost half of the children are currently enrolled within the Jewish education system.

As in the previous analysis of variance, the most powerful factor is the combined variable: intermarriage/denomination. Endogamous families (both parents are Jewish) who are Orthodox are by far more likely to provide Jewish education for their children than other types of families. For this group, in fact, an overwhelmingly majority, 88 percent, are currently enrolled in the Jewish education system. And there is a big gap between the Orthodox and those endogamous families that are Conservative, which represent the general mean with 46 percent. Those Conservative families are quite similar in terms of children's Jewish education to endogamous Reform families, for whom the figure is 48 percent. As with synagogue membership, exogamous Orthodox and Conservative and No-denominational families resemble each other, with very low proportions, about 3 percent, currently providing Jewish education for their children. Interestingly, the rate is higher for exogamous Reform families, about 17 percent.

The Jewish education of the parent is important and adds to our model. Par-

Table 5.8 Multiple Classification Analysis: Current Jewish Education of the Focal Child

Variable/category Grand Mean=.46	Effect	N
1. Intermarriage/Denomination	beta=.35	
Endogamous/Orthodox	.42	186
Endogamous/Conservative	0.00	232
Endogamous/Reform	.02	314
Endogamous/No Denomination	−.12	44
Exogamous/Conservative+Orthodox	−.44	54
Exogamous/Reform	−.29	119
Exogamous/No Denomination	−.43	48
2. Place of Residence	beta=.02	
National (excluding N.Y.)	.02	235
Greater New York	−.01	762
3. Jewish Education of Parent	beta=.06	
Yes	.02	745
No	−.07	252
4. Age of Oldest Child	beta=.19	
6–9	.08	320
10–14	.10	371
15–17	−.20	306
Multiple R Squared = .154		

ents who themselves have received Jewish education are more likely than those who never received any Jewish education to provide Jewish education for their children. While those differences are not large once we control for the other variables, they are statistically significant. The age of the focal child is also an important factor. Between the ages of 6 and 14 children are more likely to receive Jewish education since these are the years of preparation and study for Bar/Bat Mitzvah. After age 15 formal Jewish education drops off drastically—20 percent below the overall average. Once one holds constant such Jewish religious variables as denomination, type of marriage, and Jewish education of the parent, as well as such demographic variables as age of the focal child, the differences between residing in or outside New York are trivial. Moreover, this geographic factor does not add a significant contribution to the model. Overall, the model explains 15 percent of the variance (Multiple R^2 = .15).

SUMMARY

New York's rich Jewish environment makes it easier to express one's cultural, religious, and social Jewishness than probably anywhere else in the United States. Hence, a Jewish lifestyle is easier to maintain in New York. In this chapter, we have investigated various child-centered Jewish activities: Jewish camp participation, Jewish education enrollment, Jewish youth group membership, and Hanukkah versus Christmas celebration, as well as synagogue membership. We found that all these behaviors involve significantly higher levels of participation in New York than elsewhere. In general, Jewish children living in New York are more exposed to and utilize the great potential of Jewish environment and educational institutions that Greater New York offers. This greater involvement in educational Jewish activities at a young age could enhance their attachment to the Jewish community as they grow older. In addition, children who are products of interfaith marriages (which are also far less common in New York) have higher levels of Jewish activity in New York than in the nation as a whole. However, when we control for background variables such as intermarriage status, denomination, age of the child, and other demographic aspects, the differences between the Jewishness of children in and out of New York disappear.

The lack of a significant effect of residing in or outside New York leads to very important conclusions. Apparently, potentially greater access to Jewish services does not necessarily make one more Jewish; our findings indicate quite clearly that not everybody in New York joins Jewish institutions. There is indeed both a greater number and a larger than average segment of committed Jews in Greater New York. These are people who support and use the vast array of Jewish institutions in Greater New York. However, these actively Jewish people do not necessarily change the behaviors of other Jews who live in New York. We found that Reform and secularized Jews tend to behave the same in New York as in any other city. They are the least likely to join a synagogue or to send their children for Jewish schooling.

Thus we learn that it is the parents and family who make the difference, not the community or the wider social environment. Parents make the decisions regarding Jewish education for their children; they decide whether to send them to Jewish youth group or summer camp, whether to join a synagogue and/or a JCC. We realize that it takes minimum numbers of Jews to support institutions, so even where parents are committed and there are too few Jews to support institutions (e.g. small towns and cities), challenges present themselves. Still, the target of influence, from the community point of view, has to be the parents, not the synagogue or any other institution. The mere existence of communal institutions does not make Jews more Jewish. It is committed people who create and support communal institutions, not the reverse.

CHAPTER 6

IT TAKES A WHOLE COMMUNITY
TO RAISE JEWISH CHILDREN

INTRODUCTION

The modern structure of the Jewish community is different from that of the past since it can no longer depend solely on the family to transmit Jewish values, due to assimilation, intermarriage, and geographic dispersion. It needs to compensate through reliance on community-based institutions such as Jewish schools, Jewish camps, Jewish youth groups, Jewish community centers, and other avenues for participation. This chapter provides a descriptive analysis and some insights on the basis of NJPS findings concerning some components of communal intervention in children's issues and their unique roles in the process of Jewish socialization. Today, more than ever, it can be said that it takes a whole community to raise a Jewish child, the communal institutions as well as the individuals—teachers, camp counselors, day-care workers, religious leaders, etc.

Consideration of Jewish education begins with a discussion of day-care and after-school programs for infants, toddlers, and young children under both Jewish and non-sectarian auspices. With more two-working-parent households than in the recent past, these institutions play a growing role in Jewish children's lives. This is followed by a section on adoptive households, since adoption is a significant and growing phenomenon in the Jewish community that has received scant consideration in most other studies. NJPS addressed the issue in some detail. Informal Jewish education is another area of increasing interest in Jewish life. Therefore, Jewish camps, Jewish youth groups, and other such activities are also studied. The discussion not only considers the rate of Jewish youth participation in these programs, but also how the programs affect Jewish socialization.

DAY-CARE AND AFTER-SCHOOL PROGRAMS
UNDER JEWISH AND NON-JEWISH AUSPICES

The Growing Need for Day Care

The discussion in chapter 3 about the issue of working mothers showed that, as part of a general societal trend, Jewish mothers are in the labor force in greater numbers than in past generations—though their participation is still lower than the rate in the general U.S. population. Barry Chiswick (1993) has found that approximately half of Jewish mothers with children under 6 and no other children in the household participate in the labor force, compared to only a quarter in 1970. The social and economic changes that have led to two-job and dual-career families also created the need for child-care arrangements. This need may be strongest for single-parent mothers who, according to NJPS data, are as likely to work outside the home for pay as married mothers (Table 3.5).

Child care may be private and informal, such as that provided by baby-sitters, relatives, friends, or live-in providers, such as au pairs or nannies. The setting could be the child's own home, the home of the provider, or some other facility. Other child care is more formally organized, such as group day-care homes, or a day-care center housed in a facility designed and staffed to service large numbers of children. A group day-care home would generally have up to twelve children, while a family day-care home usually has only up to five children. Day-care services can be under Jewish or non-Jewish auspices. Most Jewish programs are under the auspices of synagogues and Jewish community centers. In recent years, day-care services at the workplace have become more popular. For older children, day-care services usually take the form of before- and after-school programs. In general, day-care supplements parental care by providing health supervision, developmental training, educational experiences, and social activities. Some services also provide programs, classes, and other events for the whole family.

Data

Because of the baby boomlet of the late 1980s, the largest age cohort of Core Jewish children is in ages 0–4 (391,000). NJPS data on use of Jewish-sponsored and non-Jewish day-care and preschool programs for children under 5 are indicated in Table 6.1. Of the children age 0–4 in Core Jewish households, 25 percent were in a day-care program, 37 percent were in nursery school or preschool, and an additional 37 percent were not attending any program. It is likely that many of the latter are the very youngest.

Nearly three-quarters of Jewish children who are in a day-care program were in a nonsectarian private program. Jewish-sponsored private day care served 17 percent of children in day care. Public day care accounted for the remaining 11 percent of our sample.

However, among older children, 120 attended regular school, including 41 percent who were in a Jewish private school; 39 percent in other private schools; and 20 percent in a public school, presumably preschool, nursery school, or kindergarten. The remaining 120 children were not in any program, and were presumably cared for by a parent, relative, friend, baby-sitter, au pair, or some other arrangement.

Day Care Issues

While the number of child-care facilities has grown in recent years, the potential for this service may not have been fully met. One may assume that a free market would

Table 6.1 Percentage of Core Jewish Children Age 0–4 by Day-Care and School Participation

										No Program***	Total
	Day Care*					Regular School**					
			Total	*Share*					*Share*		
	Private	*Private*	*Day*	*in*		*Private*	*Private*	*Total*	*in*		
Public	*Jewish*	*Secular*	*Care*	*Day*	*Public*	*Jewish*	*Secular*	*School*	*Regular*		
N=9	N=14	N=58	N=81	*Care*	N=24	N=49	N=47	N=120	*School*	N=120	N=321
11.1	17.3	71.6	100.0	25.2	20.0	40.8	39.2	100.0	37.4	37.4	100.0

Note: This chart represents the 391,000 Jewish children age 0–4.
*Includes any formal day-care program in a day-care center, other institutions, or home environment.
**Includes nursery and preschool.
***Including care by a parent, baby sitter, relative, friend, or live-in provider.

automatically respond by creating more child-care services if there is an unmet need. However, this assumption does not consider mitigating factors that may preclude some parents from utilizing existing services. These may include issues of affordability, location, convenience, and quality of service. While labor-force involvement is one factor in the decision to enroll children in day care, "many parents have become convinced of the importance of earlier educational and social opportunity for their preschool children. Demographic and labor force projections suggest that non-relative care will continue to grow in its share of child care supply" (Lubeck 1988, 7).

Federal funding for child-care services is likely to decrease. Although public day care is more dependent on federal funds than secular private or Jewish private day care, according to Berger (1988), about 25 percent of the Jewish programs identified government assistance as a source of funding. Jewish Federation and United Way funds extensively support Jewish day care, but user fees comprise the biggest share of support. High cost often precludes participation by poor Jews, including many single-parent families.

Considering this heavy reliance on user fees, Berger (1988) suggests that a major emerging issue will to be how to adequately serve families—particularly those of low income and single-parent families—who cannot afford the full fees. He suggests the need to establish a better balance between budget balancing and service.

The success of Jewish day care clearly rests on enabling parents of young children to work, while at the same time having their children adequately supervised. Since only 17 percent of Jewish parents with children in formal day care utilize a program under Jewish auspices, issues of affordability, availability, and accessibility have to be addressed by the Jewish community. A rational social policy would recognize this as a key area for communal investment since it could potentially secure the early affiliation of many young families. Further research on this issue would be valuable.

ADOPTIVE FAMILIES

There has been very little research on adoption among American Jews. Yet this is an intriguing topic to investigate since it sheds light on aspects of socialization of children in this population. NJPS provides a unique opportunity to explore this issue in some depth. According to the Talmud, "Scripture looks upon one who brings up an orphan as if he had begotten him" (Sanh. 19b; Meg. 13a). "There is no halakhic objection to the adopter calling the adopted child his son and the latter calling the former his father" (Sanh. ibid; based on 2 Sam.21:8, in *Encyclopedia Judaica*). Throughout Jewish history, foster care and adoption have been seen in a positive light. A strong value is placed on the adult who nurtures and educates a child, whether or not that parent gave birth to that child. Modern Hebrew for "adopt" is *ametz*, which literally means "strengthen." The etymology of this word traces back to Psalm 80, which refers to a stem of a tree being transplanted and made strong. The biblical quote, "He makes the barren woman dwell in her house as a joyful mother of children" (Psalm 113) and the oft-cited commandment, "Be fruitful and multiply," underline the pronatalist stance of the Jewish tradition. Therefore, while infertility is a difficult situation for any couple, the pain is intensified for Jews by the constant reminder of the high value Jews place on children. Adoption is one way to nurture the growth of Jewish families.

Dimensions of Adoption

Parents adopt children for a variety of reasons, but today adoption usually occurs when one of the parents is infertile. In addition to wanting a child, altruism and ideological commitment may prompt some parents to adopt. Couples with this type of motivation may cite population control and finding a home for children who are difficult to place (often mixed-race, older, or handicapped), or the desire to have a multicultural family as reasons for adopting. Single adults wishing to start a family have increasingly chosen to adopt. More often than not, however, adoptive parents do not consider the act of adopting an alternative means of creating a family, but simply choose to adopt rather than remain childless.

In her report, Gail Lipsitz states that "problems with infertility are motivating Jewish couples toward adoption. . . . [The proportion of Jewish couples struggling with infertility] is somewhat higher than in the general community, as Jews tend to marry and begin child-rearing later. Thus, although Jews are adopting for other reasons, infertility is the primary impetus" (Lipsitz 1991, 222).

Older age for marriage is associated with infertility. For this reason, the problem of infertility should be more pronounced than it was in earlier generations. The 1970 NJPS indicated that nearly half of all Jews were married by age 25. According to the 1990 NJPS, the average age for first marriage for Jewish men is 29 and for Jewish women 26. The National Center for Health Statistics reports that the median age for first marriage for all Americans is 26 for men and 24 for women (*Statistical Abstract* 1994, 103). Infertility is, then, a greater issue for Jewish couples in the 1980s and 1990s than it was earlier.

Historically, American Jews were early and efficient users of contraceptives. They have in the past and continue to make a very clear distinction between sex and pro-creation. They stand only eleventh out of twenty-three groups in their approval of an unmarried woman having a child, as indicated in the National Survey of Family and Households (NSFH).[21] Yet according to the same survey, Jews were the most likely group of all to agree that, "It's better for a person to have a child than go through life childless." They were more favorable to procreation even than the non-Christians (Muslims, Hindus, etc.), Christian fundamentalists, and Mormons. Jews tend to con-sider children important to a marriage, so that while Jews have, on average, smaller families than Christians, they have proportionately fewer involuntary childless couples.

What We Know from NJPS

NJPS includes information about twenty-eight households with adopted children.[22] Only people in households with women of childbearing age (18–44) were asked if they had adopted children. While the small sample size makes it difficult to describe the characteristics of adoptive families, some patterns emerge from the data.

The twenty-eight households containing at least one adopted child constitute 3.4 percent of the total sample of households with women in the 18–44 age group and 4.1 percent of the households with children. Of the twenty-eight households, sev-enteen have just one adopted child, ten have two, and one has three adopted children. Some of the households identified with adopted children also include children born to one or both of the parents present. The adoptive households include a total of forty adopted children and sixteen biological children. If weighted, this translates to nearly 40,000 adopted children under age 18 in Core Jewish households, representing slightly more than 2 percent of the child population.

NJPS adult respondents were asked to indicate their relationships with the other members of their households. Nearly all respondents who were adoptive parents re-ferred to an adopted child simply as their son or daughter, and did not volunteer adop-tive status until specifically asked.

In virtually all the families, the household structure was that of a traditional nu-clear family, that is, a husband and wife with one or more children. In four of the households, an additional adult or adults were also present. A much higher propor-tion of households with adopted children are in fact married couples than are all other households with children. This undoubtedly reflects the fact that some states require adoptive parents to be married.

Demography and General Characteristics

The National Council for Adoption in 1993 reported that in the late 1980s and early 1990s slightly more than 50,000 adoptions occurred each year in the United States. NJPS cannot provide precise details as to the number of Jewish adoptions that occur each year. Nevertheless it can be estimated that, since there were forty adopted chil-dren out of about a total of 1,000 children identified in NJPS (4.0 percent) and there were about 78,000 Jews under age 1 in Jewish households in 1990, then assuming in-fants were predominant, approximately 3,000 babies may have been adopted in 1990 by Jewish couples or individuals. If correct, this means that about 6 percent of children adopted in the United States in 1990 were adopted into Jewish households. Since disproportionate infertility and late marriage contribute to a greater need for adoption among Jewish couples, this overrepresentation is not surprising.

The small number of Jewish households containing adopted children in the NJPS sample are geographically distributed much like other young Jewish couples with children in the United States, with nearly half in the Northeast, just over 20 percent in both the South and the West, and just over 10 percent in the Midwest. Adoptive couples or individuals may be slightly older than other heads of households. Females 18–44 in households with adopted children have an average age of 39; the average age of males is 42. For all households that contain females age 18–44 and children of any description, the average age for females is 37 and for males 39. This tendency for adoptive couples to be somewhat older may reflect declining fertility with age as well as the added years attempting to produce children. In fact, as previously noted, NJPS may have underestimated the cases of adoptive parents because of the exclusion of households with women over 44 years old. The long-term process and waiting period associated with adopting could also contribute to the older age of adoptive parents.

A positive relationship exists between financial status and adoption. The adoptive parents' average household income is about $80,000 per year, as compared to $62,000 for all households that contain a female age 18–44 and children of any description. Since adoption is costly, the more secure financial status that generally comes with age may also be a component in the tendency of adoptive parents to be older.

Jewish Identity of Parents and Children

As with other NJPS households, the variety of definitions of Jewishness—JCOR, JNR, etc.—are present among the households that contain adopted children. Only seven of the twenty-eight households with adopted children are comprised of a married couple where both parents are Jewish by religion and born Jewish. Four couples are conversionary, comprising a Jew by religion and birth and a Jew by choice. Seven of the couples are interfaith, made up of a Jew and a gentile. The remaining ten adoptive households fall into other categories of Jewishness, such as both spouses being Jewish by choice, or Jewish with no religion.

As would be expected, in the eleven households where both parents are Jewish, all of the adopted children are being raised as Jews. In the seven cases where only one parent is Jewish, two are raising the children as Jews, three are raising the children as Christian or other religion, one is raising the children in a mix of religions, and one is raising the first child Jewish and the second child in another religion. This approximates the overall distribution on interfaith couples, covered by NJPS, just under one-third of whom are raising their children in the Jewish religion.

Of the twenty-eight families with adopted children, nine are Reform, five are Conservative, and one is Orthodox. The remaining are classified as having no denomination, something else, or another religion. This tendency toward nontraditional forms of Jewishness reflects the nontraditional outlook of many young Jewish couples found in NJPS. Also, more traditional Jews marry at an earlier age, and may therefore be less likely to confront infertility, the situation that often triggers adoption.

Most of the forty adopted children identified in the survey were U.S. born, but nine were born in Korea and other Asian countries. This again is consistent with general U.S. data. The National Council for Adoption reported that in 1992 the largest number of foreign-born adopted children were from Korea (Seader 1993, 13–a). When asked in NJPS, "In what religion was your child born?" most of the Jewish adoptive parents answered "Jewish." Yet we know that few babies available for adoption are of Jewish ethnic or religious background. While verification of Jewish religion or ethnicity at birth is not possible in NJPS analysis, we may conjecture that although adoptive parents are aware of the cultural and religious differences of their adoptive children, they nevertheless regard their children as Jewish when they adopted them as infants. Only one of the adopted children in our sample had been formally converted to Judaism. We should note that, as the adopted children grow older, more conversions may take place.

Social Service Aspects and Implications

Information collected in NJPS on the use of social services indicated that about 6 percent of all households had at some time sought help in adopting a child. This percentage is even higher if we eliminate younger age cohorts in our survey population. We may also conjecture that many more Jews would adopt if the process were easier. The high cost, extensive waiting periods, unfamiliarity with available services, concern over invasion of privacy, anxiety over potential legal problems, and emotional frustration are often cited as reasons why some couples do not seek to adopt or drop out during the process.

Data from the Association of Jewish Family and Children's Agencies (AJFCA) (1993) suggest that a small number, perhaps up to a few hundred adoptions each year, are fully planned and arranged through their constituent agencies. The majority of adoptions by Jewish adoptive households are thus handled through non-Jewish agencies, private enterprises, or other means. The Association also indicates that in the 1993 survey of the approximately 140 Jewish family and children agencies in the United States and Canada, thirty-four of the ninety-five agencies responding indicated that they provided some type of adoption services. Of these thirty-four, most offered the complete range of adoption services—infertility counseling, home studies, and other profamily support services. International arrangements for adoption were also handled by many of these agencies.

Cultural Role of Adoptees and the Role of the
Organized Jewish Community

How do these adopted children fit into American Jewish society? Those foreign-born children adopted by Jewish families in the United States who are physically and perhaps culturally different from other Jewish children. They may have a special problem fitting in. Jewish adoptive parents face the challenge of integrating their child's biological, ethnic, racial, cultural, and religious background with that of their own family. Religious issues such as *brit* (circumcision) and conversion also need to be addressed, and as the child gets older, peer acceptance issues may arise. Ethnically and socially integrated neighborhoods, schools, and social networks are important for families with cultural diversity. As non-normative, adoptive, single-mothers-by-choice, and other Jewish family types have grown in numbers, greater acceptance of these differences may occur. The organized Jewish community needs to begin educating the Jewish public to its growing variations and to deemphasize the differences of adopted children, particularly those who are of minority cultures and ethnicities.

Jewish communal institutions such as Jewish family services, Jewish community centers, Jewish schools, synagogues, as well as self-help and support groups have a role to play in facilitating the short- and long-term adjustment of adopted children. They can also serve as advocates, encouraging and supporting adoption in the Jewish community. Not only are adoptive families a growing segment of the population, but they also enrich Jewish diversity.

PARTICIPATION IN JEWISH CAMPING

Jewish camping originated a century ago in the need to remove poor immigrant children, for short periods, from overcrowded and unhealthy slum conditions. Later camps tended to become ideologically based, imbuing young people with a particular religious, social, or political orientation. They have gained a new mission in recent years, the role of a surrogate community. According to Rabbi Michael Swarttz, a former director of Camp Ramah in New England, "(Jewish) camps have been and continue to be one of the most powerful forces for Jewish continuity on the American Jewish educational scene. No other educational setting has such a 'captive audience' for an extended time period removed from the many distractions of the outside world. No other educational setting can provide an experience of total immersion in an organic Jewish community as the camp can. No other educational setting has rabbis and Jewish educators serving not only as teachers, but as sports and waterfront specialists or Israeli dance instructors. No other educational setting is able to utilize these activities not only for fun and recreation, but as vehicles to teach Jewish concepts and values" (1993, 7A). Clearly, Jewish camps can draw children closer to their Jewish culture, heritage, religion, and sense of peoplehood.

A camp can be defined as a day or overnight facility that is primarily oriented toward children, where recreational, educational, and other types of activities occur. True to their roots, most camps still function during the summer, and there is usually a strong association with athletic competition and outdoor activities such as baseball, water sports, hiking, and overnight stays in bunks and tents.

The definition of a "Jewish camp" is more problematic. Participants in a camp may be mostly or all Jewish, but this does not make it a Jewish camp. A typical Jewish camp has events, activities, and cultural themes associated with Jewish practice, holidays, and life cycle, and is usually under the sponsorship or auspices of a Jewish institution such as a JCC or a particular youth organization or denominational move-ment. Often considered the chief avenue for informal Jewish education, some Jewish camps weave Jewish rituals, symbols, and teachings into the daily routine. The use of Hebrew, incorporation of Israel-oriented programs, and the mixing of Jewish spiritu-ality with fun all foster this informal educational environment. Travel camps for teens, especially those that visit Jewish sites, as well as camps in Israel add to the variety of camp possibilities.

Using a broad parameter that allowed respondents to define for themselves what they considered to be a Jewish camp, NJPS data from Table 6.2 show that about 17.5 percent, or about 203,000 Jewish children, had participated in a Jewish camp pro-gram in the period 1989–1990. NJPS did not include data on Jewish participation in nonsectarian camps. Many of the youngest children are not yet ready to participate in a camping experience, and only 5 percent of those aged 0–4 attended a Jewish camp. However, for all other child age cohorts, between 22 and 26 percent participated in a Jewish camp.

For all age groups, children from households with higher incomes are more likely to attend than others. However, parents earning less than $20,000 a year are more likely to send their children to a Jewish camp than those in more moderate ranges. The reason is that poorer Jews, or those from single-parent families, receive camp subsidies from the community. Also, some camp programs, particularly day camps, are an inexpensive alternative to other summertime activities, such as travel.

PARTICIPATION IN JEWISH YOUTH GROUPS

Jewish youth groups also play a key role in Jewish socialization. As with camps, Jew-ish youth groups are supported or sponsored by synagogues and other Jewish institu-tions or organizations. Private secular organizations like the Boy Scouts, and public institutions like high schools, sometimes also sponsor specifically Jewish units or groups. Jewish youth groups can be religious, Zionist, or mainly social. Institutions associated with specific philosophical, social, or political ideologies such as the Re-

Table 6.2 Percentage of Core Jewish Children Who Belonged/Participated in Selected Jewish Activities by Age

Age	Jewish Youth Group N=991	Jewish Camp N=991	JCC Membership N=315	JCC User (non-member) N=239
0–4	1.0	5.1	20.4	9.7
5–9	7.7	21.8	23.5	14.7
10–14	25.1	26.4	29.5	15.4
15–17	28.3	21.6	23.8	14.3
Average of Attendees of all ages	12.6	17.5	24.1	13.3

form, Conservative, and Orthodox movements, Hadassah (Young Judaea) and B'nai Brith (BBYO) sponsor popular groups.

Approximately 12.5 percent of the Core Jewish children belonged to a Jewish youth group in 1989–1990 (see Table 6.2). This translates to about 146,000 children. Participation is most common for children age 10 and older; 25.1 percent of the 10- to 14-year-olds belong to a Jewish youth group. A larger proportion, 28.3 percent, of Core Jews age 15–17 belong to a Jewish youth group.

Jewish Community Center/YM-YWHA Participation

Jewish community centers and Ys (hereafter referred to collectively as JCC's) often feature sports and athletic competition, dance classes, art instruction, holiday parties, day care, educational workshops, discussion groups, entertainment events, camp pro- grams, youth groups, and other opportunities for social interaction. Because JCCs are community-based institutions that lack a denominational connection, they appeal to Jews from all backgrounds.

The strong correlation seen in chapter 3 between the presence of children in the household and membership in a synagogue also holds true for JCC membership. Slightly over 17 percent of all Core Jewish households maintain a JCC membership, but 24 percent of Core Jewish households that include children are currently JCC members. This translates to nearly 280,000 children. The high percentage is due to the youth-oriented activities that most JCCs provide. An additional 155,000 Core Jewish children utilize a JCC or participate in its activities, but are not members. Thus, more than a third of Jewish children have some degree of exposure to a JCC in a given year.

Table 6.2 shows that households with children age 10–14 are most likely to be JCC members; nearly 30 percent are. As for specific age cohorts, close to 175,000 teens and preteens (ages 10–17) and about 139,000 5- to 9-year-olds utilize a JCC either as members or nonmembers annually.

In his report based on NJPS, "JCC's and Jewish Identity: Confirming the Con- nection," Ed Kagen found a positive correlation between JCC membership and other Jewish behaviors. He also found a positive but weaker association of Jewish behaviors with nonmembers who utilize JCC facilities. For example, 86 percent of JCC mem- ber households where children are present also belong to a synagogue; 39 percent of nonmember users belong, while only 31 percent of nonmember/nonusers belong to a synagogue.

SUMMARY

With the increase in single-parent families and the ever-growing numbers of mothers in the workplace, day care has emerged as a significant social need. Our data indicate that the greatest usage of social services for Jewish households is in the area of infant and child day care. There is great potential for further development here, as only 17 percent of Jewish households with children indicate that they use a day-care service under Jewish auspices. The practical issue here is the penetration of the day-care market through public relations, publicity, adequate funding, and providing easy availability and accessibility. Through early participation in Jewish day care, further formal connections can emerge to the Jewish community. For this reason, as well as for its own merit, it is in the interest of the Jewish community to provide those social services that meet the needs of families, particularly those raising young children, because this will begin to cement their ties with communal institutions.

Jewish families have a greater propensity to adopt than the general population, and NJPS data indicate that there is a large number of Jewish families who are potentially interested in adoption but have not adopted. Jewish social service agencies may wish to prioritize adoption, especially in light of the current concern about low Jewish fertility. Further, the data on social services show that the greatest unmet need is assistance with adopting a child. Interestingly, adoption was the issue for which potential clients were most likely to contact a Jewish agency rather than a secular one. Despite the diverse racial and ethnic background of children adopted by Jewish families, the majority of these children are being raised as Jews. The differences in racial and ethnic background of adoptees suggest that the Jewish community needs to be open toward the multiracial background of some of its youngest members.

Summer camps under Jewish auspices present the opportunity for informal and experiential Jewish education and leisure activity that develop Jewish identity. This, of course, depends upon the character of the camp as well as the background of the family. Linking participation in informal Jewish education during childhood and teen years with adult behavior is a challenge for researchers and of interest to educators and communal leaders. Bruce Phillips (1997) correlated marriage patterns with formal and nonformal Jewish educational activities. Of the various types of nonformal Jewish education, two or more years of Jewish sleep-away camp, two or more years of a Jewish youth group, and Israel trips during the teen years were found to be associated with a marked reduction in mixed marriage. These findings support the claim that early socialization through informal Jewish educational involvement can influence childhood and teenagers' friendships and dating behavior which will in turn influence the marriage decision.

The data on JCCs reveal a strong correlation between membership in a JCC and other Jewish memberships and associational patterns or practices. This was especially true for child-centered holidays such as Hanukkah and Purim. For those households that are not members, but participate in JCC activities, the association was not as strong, yet it was still significantly stronger than those for families who neither belonged nor participated.

Youth groups have similar potential for Jewish affiliation and socialization. Adolescent development is closely associated with participation in youth groups. Though they do not reach as many youth as Jewish camps or JCC activities, Jewish youth groups contribute to the development of Jewish peer bonds and social circles, helping move youth from the social dependency of parents to that of peers.

Adolescence is an exploration stage in which young people play roles and try out for parts they wish they could play for real. Adolescence is also viewed as a psychosocial moratorium. During this period a young person "through free role experimentation may find a niche in some section of his society, a niche which is firmly defined and yet seems to be uniquely made for him" (Erikson 1968, 156). Directing adolescents to find the "niche" by opting for Jewish role models and by instilling in them a genuine sense of who they are will have positive outcomes in the long run. This genuine sense of identity is what "keeps our feet on the ground and our heads up to an elevation from which we can see clearly where we are, what we are, and what we stand up for" (Erikson 1997, 110).

Furthermore, "the reliability of young adult commitments largely depends on the outcome of the adolescent struggle for identity" (Erikson 1997, 72). Identity, according to Erikson, emanates from affirmation of childhood identifications and from the way the community identifies young individuals. "The community, in turn, feels recognized by the individual who cares to ask for such recognition" (Erikson 1997, 72). As young Jewish adolescents search and struggle to form their own identity, the Jewish community needs to provide them with rich educational and social institutions that will serve as a support system and channel their needs and interests for recognition and affiliation.

Jewish education, whether experiential or academic, which may occur in Jewish day care, Jewish camps, Jewish youth groups, JCCs and other Jewish facilities, all may enhance Jewish identity. Further research is needed to see what types or styles of Jewish education have the most enduring impact. Another area for research is how parents and children negotiate participation in Jewish-sponsored leisure activities. If more is known about this process then participation levels could be raised. The reason for this is that the support of all these leisure institutions can help ensure Jewish continuity.

CHAPTER 7

POPULATION PROJECTIONS FOR U.S. JEWISH CHILDREN

INTRODUCTION

We have, so far, described and analyzed the Jewish child population and child-related issues as of 1990. However, the NJPS also allows us to make projections from the 1990 data to the years 1995 and 2000. This is useful because there is still no source of accurate figures for the Jewish population beyond 1990. In the coming years, NJPS 2000 will shed light on the validity of these population projections. Until then, these projections should prove helpful to social, welfare, and education institutions concerned with the structure and size of the Jewish child/adolescent populations.

This chapter assesses possible trends in the Jewish child population over the coming years. Such projections are admittedly based on several assumptions that make forecasting precarious. However, they do illustrate possible developments in the size and structure of the child population under a variety of scenarios based upon current fertility patterns, and changes in what is regarded as a critical issue, the rate of interfaith marriages. Such projections are valuable to enable the Jewish community to meet the needs of children. The projections are consistent with recent studies of Jewish fertility, mortality, and marriage trends.

THE POTENTIAL JEWISH CHILD POPULATION IN 1990

We divide the child population of Core Jewish parents into two groups.[23] The first consists of children living in households where all the members are Jewish; the second consists of children living in mixed-faith households. These are households in which a related member is not a Core Jew. The latter type is usually the result of intermarriage, but could be a blended family with non-Jewish children from previous marriages, a non-Jewish stepparent, or other relatives living in the household who are not Core Jews. We excluded from this group non-Jewish household members who are nonrelatives. For this analysis the first group is named an all-Jewish household, and the second group is categorized as a mixed household. The two groups of children being analyzed in this chapter are not necessarily the same as those discussed in prior chapters. In earlier sections we were concerned with Core Jewish children and children of mixed background. Here we include non-Jewish children in households with Core Jewish children, as well as children in households with non-Jewish and Jewish relatives living in the household. Further, we expanded the cohorts to age 19. This is done to keep similar five-year age groups in the population projections; hence the oldest age group is 15–19 years old.

Overall, we find 773,000 children in the mixed-household group and 799,000 in the all-Jewish household group, according to NJPS in 1990 (see Figure 7.1). A large disparity between the two groups is found in the youngest age group, those ages 0–4. Fifty-six percent of these preschool children live in mixed households, as a result of the high incidence of mixed marriages since 1985. The youngest age group is also relatively large (almost 500,000). Their mothers belong to the large cohort of baby boomers born between 1945 and 1964. The fertility rate of these women is below replacement, yet the sheer number of mothers and delayed child-bearing contribute to the large number of babies. Children ages 5–9 are also a relatively large group (over 437,000), presumably for the same reason. We find fewer children ages 10–14, and even fewer in the 15–19 age group. These last two groups apparently reflect the lower number of women of child-bearing age rather than changes in reproductive behavior. Once again, it is worth noting that in the age categories over four, there are more children in all-Jewish than in mixed households, confirming the lower prevalence of mixed marriages in earlier years.

The Jewish children and adolescents of 1990 are the basis of our population projections for 1995 and 2000. Going beyond these years into the future would result in less accurate projections, since the assumptions underlying the model (see following page) are not as likely to be correct, especially since we assume fixed rates. For instance, we are aware of developing demographic patterns such as shifts in the age of marriage, rises in divorce rates, fluctuations in the rate of remarriage, and geographic shifts, all of which were discussed in previous chapters. But all of these might very well fluctuate. Another problem is that Jews in the United States live in an open society,

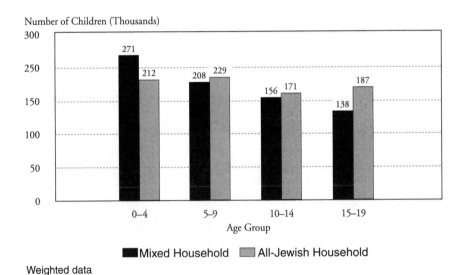

Number of Children (Thousands)

Weighted data

Figure 7.1 Child Population in 1990: Children of Core Jewish Parents

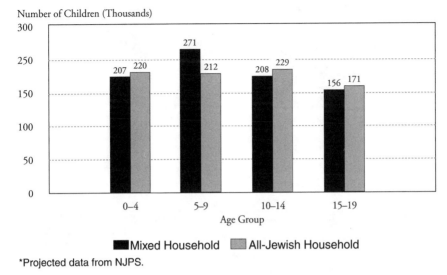

Number of Children (Thousands)

*Projected data from NJPS.

Figure 7.2 Child Population in 1995: Children of Core Jewish Parents*

and are exposed to shifts in the larger society. From the Jewish point of view, one of the most serious concerns about the next generation is the rising rate of intermarriage. As we saw in chapter 4, intermarriage tends to weaken the Jewishness of families, particularly among the younger generation. But the proportion of interfaith and interethnic marriage rates vary with changes in intergroup relations, such as the rise or decline in prejudice. Since the end of World War II acceptance of Jews has increased. If we assume that this positive community-relations environment will continue, intermarriage will not be discouraged by prejudice, but will remain an autonomous individual decision. But that too might be a false assumption.

We begin with a population projection for the year 1995 that reflects only demographic factors, namely births and deaths, leaving rates of intermarriage constant at 1990 levels. In other words, we deal with biological rather than social forces. As a result of ignoring intermarriage, this first scenario undoubtedly overestimates the number of children living in all-Jewish households and underestimates the number of children living in mixed households. The composition of the Jewish child population in the two types of household is presented in Figure 7.2.

First let us look at the potential number of mothers in the two categories, those living in all-Jewish households and those living in mixed households.[24] Overall, the total number of women of childbearing age is higher among women living in all-Jewish households, 489,000; 460,000 women are living in mixed households (see Figure 7.3). We chose to compare only women ages 15–35, since they would be the potential mothers for the following five years, and not the older women who are aging beyond childbearing years. Women in all-Jewish households outnumbered women in mixed households in every age cohort we examined except for age 25–29. This one exception may be due to a high rate of intermarriage in the cohort—note that the in-

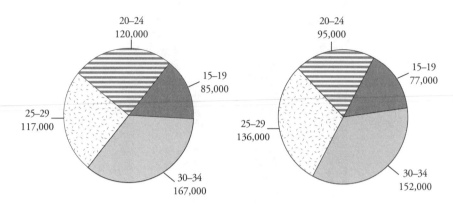

Living in All-Jewish Households   Living in Mixed Households

Figure 7.3 Women of Childbearing Age in 1990

termarried women in the survey include both Jewish women and non-Jewish wives of Jewish men.

Given the slight preponderance of women in all-Jewish households, one might expect that more children would be born to women in such households than to women in mixed households. This is a valid bio-demographic assumption, but a very unrealistic sociological one. That is because many of the women in all-Jewish households are single and a large share of them can be expected to intermarry, thus moving into the category of mixed households.

ASSUMPTIONS OF THE DEMOGRAPHIC PROJECTION MODEL

We now return to a purely demographic issue. Generally, Jewish women have very low fertility rates, which is partly explained by their high levels of education (Goldschei-der 1993; Goldstein 1992) and their older ages at marriage. The 1990 NJPS indicates that Gentile women married to Jews have similar educational levels and, therefore, similar fertility rates to Jewish women. Pepper (1995) showed convergence in the fertility patterns for women in endogamous and exogamous marriages for the years 1985–1990. There are also good reasons to assume that mortality levels are similar to those in the overall white population (Goldstein 1993).

The demographic model we use involves three factors: fertility, mortality, and immigration. These factors are the essential components of population growth and decline. The levels or rates are defined as follows:

Fertility: For women in both all-Jewish and mixed households: total fertility rate TFR=1.9.[25] For each age group, the same age-specific fertility rate was applied to each set of women, those in all-Jewish households and those in mixed households.

Mortality: The estimated life expectancy at birth is 72.6 years for males and 79.3 years for females in 1990.[26] The same mortality levels and life table (West Model) were applied to the two subpopulations (all-Jewish and mixed households).

Immigration: We assume no immigration in this model.

The above assumptions and the age structure of women of childbearing age would generate the newborns, ages 0–4, in the year 1995.

PROJECTED CHILD POPULATION: 1995—DEMOGRAPHIC AND SOCIOLOGICAL SCENARIOS

Demographic Scenario: Biological Factors Only

We begin by exploring the role of biological factors alone. To do so, we make the unrealistic assumption that no further intermarriages would occur between 1990 and 1995. This hypothetical projection points to a decreasing number of Jewish newborns in 1990–1995. Overall the Jewish population is characterized by small families. The number of children 0–4 drops from 483,000 in 1990 to 427,000 in 1995. This 12 percent decrease is based on the assumption of continuing low rates of fertility among all women: 1.9 children, below the replacement level of 2.1 children.

However, the number of women of childbearing age is larger among women living in all-Jewish households. Hence—again, given the assumption of no further intermarriage—the composition of the projected number of children 0–4 in 1995 changes: 220,000 children living in all-Jewish households and only 207,000 children living in mixed households. This suggests that even in a "no further intermarriage model,"[27] 48 percent of the children 0–4 are projected to be in mixed households. Nevertheless, the proportion in mixed households is lower than the rate of 1990 (57 percent). The projected number of children 5–9 in 1995 is the number of 0–4 in 1990: 271,000 children in mixed households and 212,000 children living in all-Jewish households. Likewise for subsequent age groups: 10–14 years old in 1995 are those 5–9 in 1990, and 15–19 years old in 1995 are those 10–14 in 1990. We are simply aging the child population by five years. This is based on the assumption that no shifts occur during the five-year period 1990–1995, namely, we expect no reclassification of the children. If the parents of these children divorce or conversion occurs and they subsequently decide to change the religious upbringing of their children, then this assumption might be invalid.

Sociological Scenario: Including Intermarriage

Once we introduce intermarriage into the model the picture changes quite dramatically. Until now, the assumption when we "age" the population has been that any teenage child growing up in an all-Jewish household would regard himself or herself as Jewish and eventually form an all-Jewish household. Clearly, this is not always the case. Today, half of all marriages involving Jews are intermarriages. There are good reasons to believe that intermarriage would continue to be a factor to the year 2000 and beyond. Thus we alter our model by allowing the all-Jewish population to lose men and women aged 15–49, the primary nuptial age as well as the primary age for women to bear children. In turn, we increase the mixed population by the same overall number of men and women. These changes are inserted into the previously cited assumptions based on fertility, mortality, and immigration.

Practically, intermarriage changes the balance between all-Jewish and mixed households in two ways. First, some of the unmarried Jewish women are intermarrying and now are in interfaith families. Second, some of the unmarried Jewish men are intermarrying and through their Gentile wives are establishing new mixed households. We provide three possible intermarriage rates over each five-year period: 40 percent, 50 percent, and 60 percent, centered on the current intermarriage rate of around 50 percent. A decrease in interfaith unions and/or increasing conversion to Judaism would conform to the 40 percent scenario; a continued rise in the intermarriage rate would support the 60 percent figure.

For population estimates incorporating the assumption of continued intermarriage, a slightly higher fertility rate is utilized, 2.1 rather than 1.9. This is in spite of the fact that fertility rates of both Jewish and Gentile women living in Core Jewish households are the same. The reason for using a higher fertility rate is somewhat subtle. It is because all of the women who enter the population under study through intermarriage are, by definition, married. Married women have a significantly higher fertility rate than unmarried women. Therefore, increasing the number of married Gentile women in a population base that includes both married and unmarried Jewish women raises the fertility rate of the group as a whole.

As a result of the increasing number of women 15–44 years old in the mixed households, the number of children in mixed households is predicted to increase beyond the previous demographic scenario. Therefore the share of these children in the overall Jewish child population would increase substantially.

In order to generate the potential mothers of 1995, we break down our population by gender, marital status, and five-year age group. Starting with age 10–14 we mature every age group by five years, so that those 10–14 in 1990 would be 15–19 in 1995, those 15–19 in 1990 would be 20–24 in 1995, and so on. Assuming that the age-specific nuptiality patterns will remain constant, the unmarried Jewish women 15–19 in 1990, who would be 20–24 in 1995, would marry at the same rate as those 20–24 in 1990. According to the 50 percent scenario, half of them would intermarry and move to the mixed-household category, and the other half would be classified as married Jewish women in 1995. The same procedure is carried out for the other age groups of unmarried Jewish women 20–24; 25–29; 30–34; 35–39; and 40–44.

In the same fashion the unmarried Jewish men would marry at the same age-specific marriage rates as men in 1990. They are then hypothetically intermarried at the given rates, and the intermarried Jewish men increase the population of women in mixed households by bringing in their Gentile wives. The new age groups of married Jewish women, married Gentile women (living in Jewish households), and unmarried Jewish women have now been created. Age-specific fertility rates of U.S. white women in 1990 are applied to all women 15–44 living in households containing a married Core Jew. Thus we obtain an estimate of the overall number of children living in Core Jewish households. For every five-year age group we then calculate the ratio between Jewish and Gentile married women in order to estimate the number of children living in all-Jewish versus mixed households. This process is repeated using first a 40 percent intermarriage rate and then a 60 percent rate.

1995 PROJECTION—THE IMPACT OF INTERMARRIAGE

Impact of Intermarriage on Child Population:
50 Percent Intermarriage

We start with 212,000 children 0–4 in the all-Jewish families and 271,000 children 0–4 years old in the mixed families in 1990. Five years later, in 1995, allowing for 50 percent intermarriage among both Jewish unmarried men and women, we get 195,000 children 0–4 in all-Jewish families and 276,000 in mixed families. Altogether, we have 471,000 children ages 0–4 living with at least one Jewish parent. This is quite similar to the overall number of children in Jewish households in 1990. However, the composition of children in the different categories changes. Due to the decrease of children in all-Jewish families, the proportion of children who live in mixed families rises to 59 percent, compared to the 56 percent figure of 1990.

Impact of Intermarriage on Child Population:
40 Percent Intermarriage

A decline in the intermarriage rate to 40 percent produces 242,000 children aged 0–4 in mixed families, and 213,000 children 0–4 in all-Jewish families. Of the 455,000 children aged 0–4 in families with at least one Jewish parent, 53 percent live in mixed families, slightly below the 1990 level.

Impact of Intermarriage on Child Population:
60 Percent Intermarriage

In this scenario we let the intermarriage rate in 1995 escalate to 60 percent. The number of children 0–4 in mixed families increases substantially to 294,000, while the number of children 0–4 in all-Jewish families drops to 182,000. Of the 476,000 children aged 0–4 in families with at least one Jewish parent, 62 percent live in mixed families.

By keeping fertility rates at replacement level the overall number of Jewish children 0–4 is maintained at the 1990 level. However, the proportion of children living in mixed families keeps on rising as intermarriage rates continue to grow.

YEAR 2000 PROJECTION—THE IMPACT OF
INTERMARRIAGE

Impact of Intermarriage on Child Population:
50 Percent Intermarriage

Allowing the three scenarios to continue to the year 2000, the number of children 0–4 in mixed households falls to 242,000, while the number in the all-Jewish households falls to 153,000. Altogether, we have a smaller number of children 0–4: 395,000, among whom 61 percent are now in the mixed families.

Impact of Intermarriage on Child Population:
40 Percent Intermarriage Rate

Allowing the 40 percent scenario to continue to the year 2000, the number of children 0–4 in mixed households is 218,000, while in all-Jewish households the number falls to 172,000. Of the 390,000 children 0–4 years old, 56 percent are in mixed families.

Impact of Intermarriage on Child Population:
60 Percent Intermarriage Rate

Continuing a 60 percent projection of the intermarriage rate to the year 2000 would mean 264,000 children aged 0–4 in mixed families and 137,000 children 0–4 in all-Jewish households. The total number of children 0–4 is 401,000. The proportion of children living in mixed families in this scenario increases substantially to 66 percent.

     This last scenario of a 60 percent intermarriage rate through the year 2000 is very alarming not only because the total number of young children living in the Jewish community decreases from almost 500,000 in 1990 to 400,000 in 2000, but because the share of children living in an all-Jewish environment shrinks to 34 percent. We must keep in mind that the assumptions in this model are not extreme. Indeed, from a demographic perspective the assumptions about the fertility rates and the incidence of intermarriage seem quite modest.

THE DECLINE IN POTENTIAL MOTHERS

In order to understand why the number of children is projected to decrease by the year 2000, we need to remember that fertility rates are fixed at replacement level and that there are reductions in the size of the cohorts of potential mothers (ages 15–44). For example, the number of married women age 25–44 will fall in every five-year age group from 1995 to 2000 in the mixed population even if there is an increase in the intermarriage rate to 60 percent (see Table 7.1 below). This is due to the replacement of large cohorts by smaller age cohorts of women of childbearing age. As the popula-

Table 7.1 Number of Married Women of Childbearing Age in Mixed Households
(60 Percent Intermarriage Scenario)

Age Group	1990	1995*	2000*
15–19	0.00	1,648	1,991
20–24	15,050	11,064	13,861
25–29	86,760	75,210	52,656
30–34	114,070	115,566	48,867
35–39	139,170	123,151	101,425
40–44	80,610	139,993	115,030
Total	435,660	466,632	333,830

*Projections.

tion ages, the baby boom generation, those born in the years 1946–64, is replaced by the "baby bust" generation, those born during 1965–79.

RAISING "EFFECTIVELY" JEWISH CHILDREN IN MIXED HOUSEHOLDS IN 1995 AND 2000

Parental choices regarding the religious identity of their children are complex in interfaith families. Raising children who are "effectively" Jewish requires parental direction and active involvement in organized Jewish life, such as Jewish education, memberships, and ritual practices at home. As shown in chapter 5, around 30 percent of children of interfaith families today are raised in Judaism. For projection purposes, in order to estimate the total number of "effectively" Jewish children in 1995 and 2000, we once again present different scenarios with regard to the religious upbringing of children in mixed households. In three scenarios, we assume that 25 percent, 35 percent, and 40 percent are raised Jewishly.

As shown in Table 7.2, the number of potential Jewish children in all-Jewish and mixed households varies according to variations in the intermarriage rate and patterns of religious upbringing. With a 40 percent intermarriage rate and 35 percent of children in mixed households raised in Judaism, the total number of "effectively" Jewish children 0–4 in 1995 would be 213,000 plus 84,700, namely 297,700. However, if the intermarriage rate is 60 percent, yet 40 percent of the children are raised Judaically, then the total number of Jewish children is projected to be 182,000 plus 117,600, or 299,600. In the latter case, although we "lose" children in the all-Jewish households, we gain more children from the mixed households.

Following the same scenarios for the year 2000 (Table 7.3), we see once more that the "losses" from the all-Jewish households could be made up by having more children raised in Judaism in mixed families. For example, in the 40 percent intermarriage scenario the total number of Jewish children may be 172,000 plus 76,300

Table 7.2 Number of Children 0–4 in 1995

| | | Children in Mixed Households | | | | Effective Range 0– to 4– |
| | | If 25% raised in | If 35% raised in | If 40% raised in | In all-Jewish | year-olds in Jewish |
Rate of Intermarriage	Total	Judaism	Judaism	Judaism	Households	Population*
40 percent	242,000	60,500	84,700	96,800	213,000	273,500–309,800
50 percent	276,000	69,000	96,600	110,400	195,000	254,000–305,400
60 percent	294,000	73,500	102,900	117,600	182,000	255,500–299,600

*The range equals column 6 plus lowest or highest number in columns 3–5.

Table 7.3 Number of Children 0–4 in 2000

| | | Children in Mixed Households | | | | Effective Range 0– to 4– |
| | | If 25% raised in | If 35% raised in | If 40% raised in | In all-Jewish | year-olds in Jewish |
Rate of Intermarriage	Total	Judaism	Judaism	Judaism	Households	Population*
40 percent	218,000	54,500	76,300	87,200	172,000	226,500–259,200
50 percent	242,000	60,500	84,700	96,800	153,000	213,500–249,800
60 percent	264,000	66,000	92,400	105,600	137,000	203,000–242,600

*The range equals column 6 plus lowest or highest number in columns 3–5.

(when 35 percent are raised Judaically), or 248,300. In the 60 percent intermarriage scenario the number of Jewish children may be 137,000 plus 105,600 (when 40 percent are raised in Judaism), for a total of 242,600 effectively Jewish children.

SUMMARY

Demographic projections for the U.S. Jewish child population show how imponderable the future is. From a demographic point of view, the range of outcomes is wide, depending on which assumptions are used. The child population potentially at risk of being included or excluded from the Core Jewish population is vast, and the actual numbers in 1995 and 2000 may be very different from those projected here if reality proves the assumptions to be wrong. Within these limits, the data suggest that the potential clientele for Jewish social or outreach programs is large. A few percentage points in the various rates makes a large difference to the actual numbers of children. Policies for inclusion or exclusion could have a dramatic long-term impact on the size of the future Jewish population. This is an immediate problem that requires careful decision making and action.

Operating within our set of assumptions, the data suggest that if current demographic patterns continue, the number of "effectively" Jewish children would decrease by about 25 percent over the next decade. Further, by 2000 as many as 60–66 percent of the children of the Jewish parents could be living in mixed families. As more divorced and more blended families emerge, it is likely that the religious composition of potential Jewish households would become less Jewish. However, this demographic model does not allow for a change in the present low level of conversion to Judaism in mixed marriages. If the proportion of Jews by choice were to rise in cases of mixed marriage, then today's 50 percent intermarriage rate could decline to a 40 percent intermarriage rate. Then, of course, the number of mixed families would fall and more Jewish families and Jewish children would result (see Tables 7.2 and 7.3).

Current discussions in the Jewish community very largely maintain that it is in the interest of all communal organizations to maximize the number of children who are raised Jewish so that the American Jewish population maintains its numbers and strength. The alternative of population decline and an aging community is seen as having negative social and morale implications. It is very doubtful that the community as a whole can succeed in having its members have more children, but it can influence the social climate in which children are raised. Hence the importance of these Jewish child population projections, which elucidate what is at stake if intermarriage rates rise or fall. Community outreach can help family decision making, particularly in socializing of young people. Interfaith families, because of their number and their ambiguous identity, are the obvious target for outreach programs. Families can ignore communal efforts by indifference, but for those who are amenable to change, institutional support to achieve inclusion within the Jewish community can expedite the process.

CHAPTER 8

CONCLUSION

FROM A COMMUNITY PERSPECTIVE

The Jewish population of the United States is diverse socially and religiously, and so are Jewish children and adolescents. Our research developed a demographic and geographic profile of contemporary American Jewish children and adolescents. It showed that overall there are 1.87 million Jewishly connected children under age 18 in 1990 and 1.16 million Core Jewish children. The large proportion of children in the lower half of the age range, 0–9 (64 percent of all children), shows that during the 1980s the Jewish population underwent a "baby boomlet." The Jewish baby boomlet will produce a correspondingly larger teenage population in the year 2000 compared to 1990. The implications from the community organizational point of view is the need for a greater supply of youth-oriented services—Jewish schools, youth groups and summer camps, Hillels, Jewish student groups, and student trips to Israel.

The religious diversity within the Core Jewish child population in 1990 is reflected in the denominational composition of their households. About two-thirds are being raised in the three main Jewish denominations: 8 percent Orthodox, 23 percent Conservative, and 35 percent Reform.[28] The growing number of Core Jewish children (26 percent) who are being raised as ethnic-cultural or secular Jews (JNR) rather than as Jews who identify themselves by religion (JBR) are less exposed to Jewish education and to synagogue attendance. Their families are generally unobservant of Jewish holidays, Shabbat, kashrut laws, and other traditional rituals. Such American Jewish children likely go with their parents to a museum more frequently than they go to a synagogue. This secularization of children's lives reflects the secular preferences of a significant proportion of younger Jewish parents, even while they continue to identify as Jews.

Yet we have to recognize that even parents who are highly committed to transmitting their Jewish heritage to their offspring face difficult challenges in today's world. Our review of the socialization literature has shown that it is very difficult to isolate children from external influences and that the parental monopoly of influence evaporates and parental control becomes attenuated on two levels. First, as children grow up, peer and extrafamilial influences grow more powerful. Second, the all-pervasive consumer society that surrounds us increasingly affects the environment of American children. The ever-present communications media and the advertising programs of corporations are more and more directed at youth markets. The sophisticated marketing of fashion in clothing, toys, foods, films, etc., uses peer pressure to help produce a highly materialistic, present-oriented youth culture which is at odds with Jewish values of spirituality, learning, tzedakah, and self-discipline as exemplified by Sabbath observance. Of course, these concerns are not unique to the Jewish population. They are shared by many other cultures in U.S. society.

Moreover, in this study, a communal perspective was adopted, focusing on the collective needs of families and socialization of children into the social group rather than dealing with family relations and individual child development. The need to reach out to the next generation of Jews, the children, is a critical task the organized Jewish community faces, given the strong value placed on communal aspirations for continuity. To accomplish this successfully, Jewish leaders, educators, rabbis and planners need to accommodate the increasingly diverse needs of Jewish children and their families. Pluralism and diversity of family types are consequences of the growing complexity of household structure in modern societies.

The organized Jewish communal institutions need to become aware of the shift from the traditional nuclear two-parent family towards single-parent and non-normative families. In 1990 over 13 percent of Core Jewish children lived in single-parent households and around 2 percent of the households with children are defined as non-normative (i.e., a particular household type that is neither single-parent nor a married-couple household). In addition, the community includes of a number of other Jewish family types: families with adopted children, intermarried families, poor families and families that are simply unaffiliated. To secure Jewish continuity and viability, all of these families and their children need to be integrated into the Jewish community. Jewish community agencies ought to consider marketing the programs and services, so they can appeal to this diverse potential constituency—for example, build and expand day-care facilities to help dual earners and single-parent families, provide services and support groups for families with adopted children, or subsidize poor families to help them become affiliated with and involved in synagogues and JCCs.

Based on our population projections developed in chapter 7, 60–66 percent of Jewish children ages 0–4 in the years 1995–2000 would live in religiously mixed households: that is, a family in which one of the adult members is a Gentile. Among children of interfaith families in 1990, only about 30 percent of children of mixed families are raised in Judaism. Remarriages and the increasing incidence of blended families further create religiously mixed households. These families consist of adults and children who observe different religions living in the same household. Such trends produce further challenges to the community's goal of retaining the next generation as self-identifying Jews and assuring their affiliation with the Jewish community.

Intermarriage appears to be inevitable in a free society, but decisions about conversion and parental choice of whether to raise children in Judaism are not. To cope with the projected trend, both religious and lay leaders must establish services and programs that help engender a strong Jewish identity in all segments of the community, including children of mixed households. The key population that must be recruited in order to help maintain the size of the next generation of Jewish children is unmarried young adults, who will be the next generation of parents. For this group, intermarriage prevention will raise the number of children in all-Jewish families. An alternative policy aimed at mixed-faith couples requires more outreach and conversion of non-Jewish spouses both before and after marriage. Success in these areas will ultimately lower the intermarriage rate. That is what is projected in the 40 percent intermarriage scenario shown in chapter 7. Policies directed toward parents and children will include outreach programs that, one hopes will persuade a larger proportion of the mixed families to raise their children as Jews. This would ultimately increase the Core Jewish population. The two types of policies, encouraging Jewish marriage and outreach to the interfaith family, are not incompatible. In fact, the organized Jewish community could opt to do both.

The problem of marking the boundaries of the Jewish population is even more complex. What of the children of intermarried Jewish parents who are being raised in no religious tradition (JNR)? Almost half these children are of course *halakhically* Jewish since the mothers are Jewish. Should they be included in our counts of Core Jews, as is the case with the current adult population? Yet beyond mere enumeration, there is the problem for the community of socializing tens of thousands of these children to a nonreligious Jewish identity.

Mixed marriage has been shown to be a component in generational trends towards assimilation. Egon Mayer concludes that, "There is little doubt that two generations of intermarriage will produce a third generation in which Jewishness is highly attenuated if it survives at all" (1994, 78). The issue of intermarriage has moved so much into the forefront that federations, JCCs, and others in the field of Jewish communal service have been devoting considerable efforts to develop strategies of outreach. Strengthening Jewish identity has been a principal component of this effort. What modes of outreach to intermarried families are acceptable and effective? What are the implications for Jewish education in serving children of intermarriage? What services can be provided to strengthen their Jewish identity? What are the political implications for federations in dealing with the intermarriage issue? And, how should limited funds be allocated to critical competing demands such as confronting the high intermarriage rate or providing programs to promulgate Judaism among children from interfaith homes?

In addition to defining these issues, we also need to recognize the diversity among interfaith couples and understand how they differ from endogamous couples. From a marketing perspective, can Jewish institutions effectively market programs that make Jewish living more desirable? Although less than a third of children of interfaith families are being raised as Jews, a significant percentage of the remainder are being raised with some exposure to Judaism, through secularized or syncretic forms of Judaism. Thus, the importance of reaching this population should not be overlooked; "Those who ignore the potential for Jewish continuity amongst the descendants of the intermarried, given the magnitude of their numbers, are also condemning hope in the American Jewish future" (Mayer 1994, 78).

An analysis of family decision making about the religious identity of children in interfaith families explored the determinants of whether children will be identified as "Jewish" in those situations when only one of the parents is Jewish by religion. Mothers enjoy a culturally bestowed authority with respect to childrearing both in American society and in Jewish tradition. It is commonly believed that they also have the primary role in defining their children's religious identity. This conventional wisdom is true when the mother has a stronger interest than the father in the outcome of the religious identity decision (viz. when she is "Jewish by religion" and he is a Gentile without religion), and is more true when the mother also enjoys status-related social resources such as higher education. Ironically this fits into a *halakhic* model, whereby in traditional Judaism, Jewish status passes down through the maternal line.

However, the multivariate analysis showed that when other factors such as degree of religiosity are held constant, mothers do not have stronger influence on children's religious identity. The religious composition of parents is the main predictor in the decision matrix regarding children's religious identity. This factor represents the relative competence and the interest in the decision of the more committed Jewish parent in raising and identifying his or her child as Jewish. The role of the status-related social resources is shown in the analysis by the importance of the level of educational attainment of the Jewish parents; the more educated Jewish parents are more likely to identify their children as Jewish. Further research is needed to determine the extent to which this same decisional matrix applies in equal measure to other facets of children's religious socialization beyond mere identification.

The uniqueness of New York as a setting for Jews in America led to a special study of Jewish children residing in New York, drawing on the rich set of data collected in the NYJPS. The exposure to a more Jewish environment seems to be a positive stimulus. However, such differences were observed only on a descriptive level; they largely disappeared once key background variables were controlled in a multivariate analysis. These results showing a lack of a significant effect from residing in New York leads to several important conclusions. While it is easier to be Jewish in New York, apparently the opportunity to interact more frequently with other Jews and to have easier access to Jewish facilities does not necessarily make one more Jewish. There is a substantial segment of committed Jews in New York, to be sure. These are special people who produce the vast Jewish institutions of Greater New York. Greater New York has more Orthodox Jews, and traditional Judaism is more supported in New York. The city also has more first-generation Americans. However, these people do not seem to change the type and strength of identity of other Jews who live in New York. Reform and secularized Jews tend to behave the same in New York as in Phoenix or other places.

The contextual analysis revealed an important finding: that for young children in particular it is the parents who make the difference, not the community. Parents make decisions regarding Jewish education for their children; they decide whether to send them to a Jewish youth group or summer camp, whether to join a synagogue and/or a JCC. This finding is consistent with what socialization theory outlined in chapter 1 predicts. The family is the primary agent for the socialization of children. Thus, a key target from the Jewish community's point of view should be the parents.

Our study explored not only how many Jewish children there are and will be, but who these children are. We project that not only will there be more children in interfaith families and more in non-normative families, but also more children in areas of low population density, and thus fewer in areas with organized Jewish life. This presents major challenges for the Jewish community. Its organizations and agencies will have to relocate programs and engage in geographical as well as social outreach. They must establish programs that encourage the participation of all types and segments of the child population in communal activities such as youth groups, educational programs, and synagogues in new and dispersed locations where Jews reside.

Involvement of parents in Jewish life requires significant sums of money for fees, synagogue dues, religious school, and Jewish camp for the children, membership in a Jewish Community Center, and annual contributions to the UJA/Federation campaign or other Jewish charities. Additional high expenditures are involved in day-school education and a Bar or Bat Mitzvah celebration, membership in a youth group and participation in a trip to Israel. Scholarships and flexible fee policies for the economically disadvantaged will have to become a more common practice for Jewish institutions if they wish to insure more equal opportunity for participation in these activities. Even though the biggest barrier to Jewish communal participation may not be financial but attitudinal, the financial burden is undoubtedly a substantial factor. Making a Jewish way of life compelling and attractive and affordable is the key to solving this problem. Unwillingness to face this issue will mean that for many parents and children, Jewish cultural deprivation and economic deprivation will be highly correlated.

What effort should national Jewish organizations make to reach Jewish children and their families in areas with little local Jewish organizational structure? How can Jewish services and institutions such as synagogues, camps, and major cultural, or religious events attract participants from distant locations? Can electronic communications, like the Internet, help connect Jews to a national community? For areas with small Jewish populations, the focus may need to shift toward programs without walls: in other words, portable services. Outreach could be coordinated on a national level, and denominational services, federations, and other Jewish organizations may need to be better connected in coordinating campaigns and delivering service.

High levels of migration among contemporary American Jews makes it less likely that three generations of Jewish families will live in close proximity. The consequence is a lack of social and religious support networks for children based on family and kin. In many families, grandparents and grandchildren live far apart. This could be offset by programs of surrogate or "foster grandparenting." Furthermore, the lack of a support system adds to the motives for having small families. Given the high proportion of dual-career and two-job families, leaders of the community need to provide more support service for parenting if they wish to encourage families to have more children. In the absence of an increase in fertility, which is now below the replacement level, in approximately thirty years the Jewish population will decline when smaller birth cohorts of women move into their reproductive years.

However, in the short term, the growing size of the teenage population at the end of the 1990s suggests that the organized Jewish community would be wise to recognize the needs to develop more effective agents of socialization for adolescents beyond the family unit, because the family is of decreasing importance for this age group. The teen years are a critical time when many choose to "drop out" of organized Jewish life. This occurs because, as earlier discussion of relevant theories suggest, teenagers characteristically challenge authority and reject many norms of their childhood years. Jewish life often narrows after religious school graduation. The Bar/Bat Mitzvah is commonly the negotiated end of the child's Jewish experience. "The result is that a significant number of adult Jews attempt to relate to their Judaism with a 13-year-old understanding of a rather complicated religious tradition" (Edelman 1993, 4).

There is a strong argument for the establishment of Jewish youth groups as agents of Jewish socialization. Because adolescence is a period of transition and quest for self-definition, there are specific means by which youth groups, movements, and camps can respond to the needs of adolescents. While the youth group's most obvious role is that of a socializing agent, a more intrinsic role is that of an identity builder. Although identity enhancement is critical in the social and educational process, the ultimate goal of most Jewish youth groups should be the creation or cultivation of the Jewish identities and Jewish circles of its members.

The youth movement can give the adolescent a solid foundation through strong bonds to the Jewish community, while being sensitive to the adolescent's desire to make personal choices, exercise control, and discover a sense of self. Moral development and Jewish identity enhancement should be key elements in all Jewish youth groups and the diversity of these groups should reflect the variety of Jewish experiences that are possible.

Our research explored an assortment of social, demographic, and economic processes among contemporary American Jewry that have direct relevance to the Jewish "welfare" of children: increasing intermarriage and divorce rates, increasing single parenthood and non-normative families, and high mobility. These recent patterns determine the size and composition of American Jewish communities. The contribution of this volume is the social profile and projections of the Jewish child population. Now that some important basic facts about the next generation of American Jews are known, it is time for the leaders and planners of the various denominations and agencies within the American Jewish community to open a debate and then respond accordingly.

Jews in America face a challenge in transmitting their Jewish heritage to the next generation. American secular culture is highly seductive. Judaism itself is a minority religion. For these reasons American Jews must use all means at their disposal to "socialize" their children into being Jewish. Traditionally, the family played the primary role in socialization, especially for younger children. However, in an era of mixed marriages and single-parent families, it is not always possible for families to carry out this role to the fullest. While the Jewish community at large cannot "socialize" children without parents' involvement, it should attempt to give more support—moral and financial—to parents in passing the torch of Jewish religion, scholarship, culture, and values to the next generation of American Jews through the further development of programs in Jewish family education.

APPENDIX

THE METHODOLOGY OF THE NATIONAL
JEWISH POPULATION SURVEY

Joseph Waksberg[29]

Large-scale sample surveys are frequently carried out in a number of discrete steps and the National Jewish Population Survey (NJPS) followed such a pattern. The steps consisted of: determination of the subjects to be included in the survey; development of specific question wording; testing questions and procedures, decisions on survey procedures; preparation for data collection, including recruitment and training of staff; sample selection; data collection; weighting and other aspects of data processing; internal analysis of potential sources of errors; tabulations; analyses and preparation of reports. This methodological report concentrates on the technical aspects relating to sampling, survey procedures and data collection, weighting, and issues relating to accuracy of the data. There is a brief description of the questionnaire development. Data analysis and preparation of publications, both of the monographs and of less detailed reports, are not part of the survey methodology and are not discussed here.

1. GENERAL SURVEY PROCEDURES

United Jewish Communities, formerly known as The Council of Jewish Federations (CJF), established and supports a National Technical Advisory Committee on Jewish Population Studies (NTAC). At the time the NJPS was planned, the NTAC consisted of researchers who worked for the CJF or local Jewish federations and outside demographers and statisticians interested in Jewish issues. The NTAC endorsed an initial recommendation of the October 1987 World Conference on Jewish Demography in Jerusalem to conduct a U.S. National Jewish Population Survey (NJPS) in the spring and summer of 1990. The CJF concurred in this recommendation and agreed to support such a survey.

The choice of 1990 was a deliberate one since it placed the survey at about the same time as the 1990 U.S. Census, thereby insuring maximum comparability between the Jewish survey data and census statistics. Further, the time period chosen for the conduct of the detailed interviews—late spring and early summer—both corresponded to the timing of the Census and is a time when most college students can be reached in their families' residences or other dwelling places that are more permanent than dormitories or other college housing. The interviewing period is also the time that most Sunbelt residents are in their more permanent homes.

The NTAC had independently come up with 1990 as the logical period for the survey as part of more general considerations of appropriate survey methodology. In a series of meetings in the decade leading up to 1990, the NTAC had discussed the many aspects of planning and implementing a Jewish Population Study and had submitted the following recommendations to the CJF:

- *That a large scale survey of the Jewish population be conducted in 1990.*
- *Data collection should be by telephone.* Over the past twenty to thirty years, survey researchers had demonstrated that the quality of responses to inquiries over the telephone were, for almost all subjects, about the same as for face-to-face interviews. Response rates to telephone surveys are generally lower than in face-to-face interviews, but the cost of telephone surveys is so much lower that the NTAC felt that the substantial cost advantage of a telephone survey more than compensated for the adverse effect on quality of a lower response rate.
- *A sample of 2,000 to 2,500 Jewish households should be selected by random digit dialing (RDD), without any use of Federation or other lists of Jewish households.* RDD gives all households with telephones in the United States (both Jewish and non-Jewish) a known chance of selection into the sample so that lists are not necessary. Furthermore, it was the NTAC's judgment that the effort involved in trying to construct a national list, and the likely small percentage of U.S. Jews that would be on the list, would make the construction of the list counterproductive. It should be noted that households without telephones were not intended to be covered in the survey. In 1990, about 7 percent of U.S. households did not have telephones. However, the percentage is undoubtedly much lower for Jewish households, and the NTAC did not believe their omission would have any detectable effect on the quality of the survey results. The survey also was to omit the nonhousehold population, principally persons in nursing homes, long-term hospital units, religious institutions, military barracks, and prisons. College students in dormitories (as well as those in private residences) were to be covered in the survey, usually as members of their parents' households.
- *Data should be collected only for the civilian population living in the households,* omitting the institutional and other nonhousehold population. The survey thus would exclude those in prisons, hospitals, nursing homes, hotels, religious institutions, and in military barracks. Estimates of the relatively small number of Jews in such places were added to the survey results for the estimate of the total number of Jews in the United States. However, their characteristics would not be reflected in the breakdowns of the totals by age, sex, etc.
- *A screening questionnaire that defines and identifies Jewish households should be administered to the sample of telephone households.* Since random digit dialing

produces a sample of all U.S. telephone households, non-Jewish households would then be dropped and Jewish households retained for the survey.

- *That the survey include a wide variety of topics.* The NTAC developed a broad set of questions designed to shed light on the demographic, social, and economic characteristics of the Jewish population, and to provide information on items of specific Jewish concern, such as intermarriage, Jewish education, philanthropy, observances of Jewish rituals and practices, synagogue membership, utilization of social services, volunteerism, attitudes to certain issues of Jewish concern, etc. The questions were divided into two groups: (a) ones for which reasonably accurate information for all household members could be provided by any adult in the household (e.g., age, education, observance, etc.) and (b) questions for which the accuracy of proxy responses would be in doubt (e.g., attitudes). For the first set of questions, data would be obtained for all members of the sample households. For the second group, the NTAC recommended that one adult be selected at random in each sample household and that the sample for these items should be considered as consisting of only the selected persons.

- A second, and independent, partition of the questions was also made. In order to reduce the considerable interview length, the questionnaire was divided into a "core" component, to be asked in all sample households, and "modules" to be asked in subsamples of households. More specifically, respondents were randomly allocated to three equal subsamples, and each subsample was assigned one of the three following areas of inquiries:

1. Jewish identity
2. Social services
3. Philanthropy

- *After the survey information was collected, weights should be inserted into the data file.* The weights should be constructed so that when they are used in tabulations of the survey data, they provide approximately unbiased estimates of the U.S. Jewish population in each category shown in the tabulations.

- *The individual responses to the survey questionnaire as well as the appropriate weights should be entered onto a computer tape.* Copies of the tape would be available for researchers interested in making detailed studies of particular aspects of Jewish life.

- *A high priority was put on speed of data processing, tabulations of the data, and publication of the major results,* first in a summary report highlighting the major findings in the survey, and then in a series of analytic studies focusing on particular topics.

- *That the survey be conducted outside of CJF or its member organizations.* More specifically, that a contract be let by competitive bidding to a company experienced in the conduct of such statistical studies.

The CJF approved the NTAC recommendations, provided a budget for the survey, and asked the NTAC to make the necessary arrangements. A Request for Proposals (RFP) that described the work to be done, the procedures outlined above, and the scope of work was prepared and distributed to interested statistical and market research companies. A subcommittee of the NTAC received the proposals submitted by organizations that were interested in carrying out the survey, and selected the ones that were judged best. These organizations were invited to make personal presentations of their plans and their experience in such activities before the subcommittee. A contract was then awarded to a team consisting of ICR Survey Research Group and Marketing Systems Group (also known as Genesys Sampling Systems). The Marketing Systems Group was responsible for the sample selection and all weighting and estimation phases of the project. ICR was responsible for all other aspects of the survey, from questionnaire pretesting through data collection, coding, and data tape preparation.

The choice of ICR and Marketing Systems Group was based on a number of factors: understanding of the requirements of the study, the reputation of the team in doing high-quality work, experience with large-scale telephone sample surveys, an existing staff of experienced telephone interviewers and a system for training and supervising them, a capable statistician to oversee the sampling and related activities, and cost. A main, and overriding advantage of the team, was the fact that they carried out, for other sponsors, a weekly RDD national household sample survey of 2,000 households. They agreed to add the screening questions that identified Jewish households to the questionnaire then in use. It was estimated that the approximately 100,000 households screened over the course of a year would supply the 2,500 responding Jewish households desired in the final sample. (The screening actually covered more than a year, and consisted of over 125,000 households which yielded over 5,000 households that indicated the presence of a Jewish member.) By attaching the screener questions to an existing national sample survey, the NJPS was able to avoid the expense of selecting and interviewing the very large sample needed to locate 2,500 Jewish households. Instead, the survey incurred only a fairly modest marginal cost of the added time to administer the screening questions. If the NJPS had to pay the entire cost of selecting and screening more than 100,000 households, the additional cost probably would have been well over $1,000,000.

An additional advantage of using the ICR's ongoing weekly survey was that it provided flexibility in achieving the desired sample size. The amount of screening necessary to achieve a sample of 2,500 Jewish households could only be approximately estimated in advance. With the weekly samples screened by ICR, a cumulative tally of Jewish households could be kept, and the weekly samples terminated before the end of the year if fewer than 100,000 households provided the required sample size, or it could be continued for longer than a year if that was necessary.

2. SAMPLE SELECTION

The telephone numbers selected for the NJPS were based on random digit dialing (RDD), and are a probability sample of all possible telephone numbers in the United

States. The sampling procedure utilized a single-stage sample of telephone numbers within known residential working banks (the first two digits of the four-digit suffix, e.g., 212-555-XXxx). Telephone exchanges were strictly ordered by census geographic variables (i.e., Division, Metro/Non-Metro, Central City/Suburban, etc.) creating a sample frame with fine implicit geographic stratification. This procedure provides samples that are unbiased and in which all telephones have the same chance of selection. Since the random digit aspect allows for the inclusion of unlisted and unpublished numbers, it protects the samples from "listing bias"—the unrepresentativeness of telephone samples that can occur if the distinctive households whose telephone numbers are unlisted and unpublished are excluded from the sample. The RDD sample is referred to as the "screening sample." It consisted of 125,813 households that were asked whether any household members was Jewish. (See Section 4 for specific questions.) All qualified Jewish households were followed up with requests for the detailed interviews.

The household sample selection was accompanied by an automated scheme for scheduling callbacks for telephone numbers at which there was no response to the initial call. A three-callback rule was followed—the timing of the callbacks was scheduled by the computer to cover various times of the day, but within a narrow time frame. This narrow time frame was required by the short field period for each weekly survey. There were actually two weekly sample surveys, with 1,000 households in each survey. One weekly survey ran from Wednesday evening through Sunday evening; the second from Friday evening through Tuesday evening. The initial call and callback schedule ensured a minimum of two week-end attempts (if necessary) on each sample number.

The tight time schedule for the screening interviews undoubtedly reduced the response rate, as compared to a survey with more time for callbacks. (For example, persons on a vacation during the survey week were never given an opportunity to respond.) However, the NTAC believed that the advantages of using an ongoing survey for screening outweighed the disadvantages.

3. PRESURVEY OPERATIONS

Two major sets of activities preceded the data collection. They consisted of the development and testing of the survey questions, and the interviewer training and briefing.

3.1. Development and Testing of Survey Instruments

Three stages of data collection were planned: screening, recontact and in-depth interviewing. The questionnaires for all three phases were initially developed by the NTAC. These documents were then edited, reformatted, and programmed for CATI interviewing by ICR staff. The development phase included several questionnaire drafts and a series of "live" pretests.

CATI stands for Computer Assisted Telephone Interviewing. It is a system in which the questionnaire has been entered into a computer, each interviewer is provided with a computer screen and keyboard, and the questions to be asked appear on the screen instead of having to be read from a paper questionnaire. The responses are entered directly into the computer. In addition to speeding up the data processing, CATI has the capability of carrying out editing for consistency and completeness of data and flexibility of operations. Almost all large-scale telephone surveys are now done by means of CATI.

All interviewing in both the Screening, Recontact/Validation, and the Main Study Phases were conducted by professional interviewers by means of computer-assisted telephone interviewing. From an interviewing standpoint, the CATI system removes the potential for interviewer error relative to skip patterns and possible response options. Moreover, the CATI system provides inherent response editing capabilities relative to both range edits and conditional requirements based upon prior responses. Computerized questionnaire control allows interviewers to better establish rapport with respondents and concentrate on responses rather than attempting to contend with the extreme complexity of the Recontact and Main Study questionnaires.

Finally, CATI capabilities allowed for access to up-to-the-minute interviewing production measures including production rates, refusal and refusal conversion rates, and results of dialing attempts.

In each pretest, personnel from NTAC and ICR monitored interviewers as they were being conducted. Any unforeseen deficiencies in question content, sequencing, and nomenclature were corrected during this stage. In most cases, indicated changes were incorporated immediately, providing pre-test capabilities during the same pretest session.

The final CATI questionnaires were reviewed and tested extensively by both NTAC and ICR personnel prior to "live" interviewing. In addition, the pretest data served as a "live" test of output, data format, edit checks, etc.

3.2. Interviewer Training and Briefing

All interviewers selected to work on the 1990 NJPS were personally briefed, trained, and supervised during all hours of interviewing. In addition to participating in the standard ICR ten-hour interviewer training session, all interviewers who worked on the survey participated in a detailed briefing session developed specifically for this study.

This special briefing included an item-by-item discussion of each question and module contained in the interview; a discussion of special respondent "handling" for specific interview situations, including providing the CJF's telephone number to respondents who questioned the authenticity of the survey and suggesting that the CJF be called; and a review of areas and issues relating to Jewish heritage including customs, holidays, and proper pronunciation of Hebrew words and phrases that interviewers would be likely to encounter during the course of the study. In addition to the briefing, written interviewer aids were provided and made available during all hours of interviewing.

4. ORGANIZATION OF DATA COLLECTION ACTIVITIES

For approximately one year preceding the survey, beginning in April 1989, ICR conducted Stage I of the National Jewish Population Survey. This entailed incorporating a series of four screening questions into its twice weekly general market telephone surveys. The screening questions determined Jewish qualification and thus were the basis for the recruitment of households. The four screening questions in Stage I were asked in the following order:

1. What is your religion?
   If not Jewish, then . . .
2. Do you or anyone else in the household consider themselves Jewish?
   If no, then . . .
3. Were you or anyone else in the household raised Jewish?
   If no, then . . .
4. Do you or anyone else in the household have a Jewish parent?

This screening stage of the survey obtained information on the religious preference of 125,813 randomly selected adult Americans and the Jewish qualification of their respective households. It was determined initially that 5,146 households contained at least one person who qualified as "Jewish" or Jewishly affiliated as determined by the screening questions. Stage II, the inventory stage, consisted of attempts to recontact Jewish households to requalify potential respondents and solicit participation in the 1990 NJPS. The households classified as Jewish in the last three months of screening were omitted from Stage II because the Stage III interviewing was to follow so closely. Stage II included 4,208 households. During Stage II, a number of households that were initially classified as Jewish dropped out of the survey sample due to changes in household composition or to disqualification based upon further review.

Stage III, the final interviewing stage of the survey, yielded a total of 2,441 completed interviews with qualified respondents. The statistics reported here are drawn from these households. Through a process of scientific weighting procedures utilizing all 125,813 Stage I interviews, the sample of Jewish households represents about 3.2 million American households nationally.

The survey interviews collected information about every member of the household. Thus, the study was able to ascertain important personal information about 6,514 persons in the surveyed households. Appropriate weighting procedures indicate that the number of persons in the surveyed households represents about 8.1 million individual Americans, a number of whom are not themselves Jewish, reflecting the mixed composition of the households in the Jewish sample.

5. DATA COLLECTION: FIRST TWO PHASES—SCREENING AND RECONTACT AND VALIDATION

5.1. Phase I: Screening

The entire screening phase was conducted as part of the ICR Survey Research Group's twice weekly telephone omnibus survey. The use of a telephone omnibus vehicle as opposed to a custom survey has obvious cost advantages; on the other side, there may be trade-offs relative to response rates, length of field period, placement of the screening questions on Jewish identity with the ever changing instrument, etc. However, these were thought to be small.

As mentioned earlier, 125,813 screeners were completed for this project. Although no formal disposition of call results is available, it is known that the proportion refusing to participate in any given weekly survey averages about 45 percent. In order to assess the potential bias resulting from this response rate, two separate analyses were conducted. They are described in Section 9.

5.2. Phase II: Recontact and Validation

The second phase of the study was conducted with respondents from Jewish households identified during the initial Screening Phase. This phase was designed to validate the initial screening process; to initiate contacts with qualified households to explain the purpose of the study and gain cooperation; and to provide a means of keeping in touch with the qualified respondents given the extended time period between the initial screening and final interview.

The primary informational objectives of the Recontact/Validation Phase were as follows:

1. Validate that the respondent/household was, in fact, Jewish;
2. Explain the purpose of the call and encourage respondents to participate in the in-depth Study during the summer of 1990;
3. Collect detailed household data relating to age, sex, and relationship of each household member, and type of residence and location; and
4. Request and secure a third party reference to assist in the future recontact for the in-depth Study.

Recontact Phase interviewing was conducted over a 52-week period, from 7 April 1989 through 2 April 1990. The process was continuous, with most recontacts occurring within two weeks of the initial qualification in the Screening Phase.

Upon successful recontact, the household member who participated in the Screening Phase was asked to reverify the Jewish character of himself/herself and other household members relative to:

• Being Jewish;
• Considering himself/herself Jewish;
• Being raised Jewish; and
• Having a Jewish parent.

Respondents were asked to participate in an in-depth Main Study Phase interview to be conducted at a later date. This recruitment included an explanation of the study, the size of the study, an explanation of how and why they were selected to participate, and the naming of CJF as the study sponsor.

Substantial efforts were made to "convert" respondents who refused to participate. Respondents who refused to participate at the introduction or during the interview itself were recontacted by specially trained interviewers. These interviewers used specially developed and proven techniques to convert refusals into participants. In some cases, alternative respondents within a given household were recruited to participate. In addition to specially trained interviewers, letters of explanation were mailed to refusals in an effort to establish credibility for the study and, in turn, to increase likely participation.

A household inventory of requalified Jewish households was created; this roster of household members included age and sex, along with each member's relationship to the primary contact person. Specifically, four questions were asked about each household member:

1. Name;
2. Age and sex;
3. Relationship to the respondent; and
4. Religious qualification.

Additional information relating to household characteristics was also requested; specifically, the type of household unit (e.g., multiple family, single unit, apartment, etc.) and whether this particular unit was the primary residence or a seasonal or similar recreational dwelling.

Finally, information about third-party references (i.e., a relative or close friend) was requested for use in the event that respondents could not be reached at their original location. This third-party information was utilized to "track" the original respondents during the final phase of interviewing.

Not every Jewish household identified in the Screening Phase was included in the Recontact Phase. Specifically, households identified during the final three months of Screening were excluded because of the rather short time until onset of the full National Survey; it was thought that the risk associated with alienating respondents by attempting multiple contacts over a very short period of time outweighed the few households likely to be lost due to relocation.

In total, 4,208 Jewish households identified in the Screening Phase were included in the Recontact Phase. The results of attempted recontact are shown in table A.1. It should be noted that there was no strict callback rule, but rather "nonrespondent households" were continually recycled, with many receiving 20 attempts or more.

Over 81 percent of the screened and qualified households were successfully contacted and reinterviewed; of these, 15.5 percent did not requalify and 6.3 percent disavowed knowledge of the previous interview. Just over 9 percent refused the Recontact interview.

None of the original respondent households were excluded from the 1990 Survey based on results of the Recontact Phase; the purpose here was to facilitate tracking of respondents and increase ultimate cooperation, not to requalify, validate, and

Table A.1 Results of the Recontact Validation Phase

	Number	*Percent*
Requalified and willing to participate	2,124	52.1
Requalified and not willing	316	7.5
Not requalified	652	15.5
No such respondent	266	6.3
Refused at start	315	7.5
Refused during interview	75	1.8
Language barrier	27	0.6
Nonworking	135	3.2
Nonhouseholds	20	0.5
No Contact	278	6.6
Total	4,208	100.0

reject sample households. Although the Recontact data were retained, all sample households (including those that failed to qualify in Phase II) regardless of the outcome were again attempted during the Final Phase of interviewing.

6. PHASE III: MAIN STUDY—DATA COLLECTION

In the spring and summer of 1990, the third and final phase of data collection was undertaken. The survey instrument itself was initially developed by the NTAC, jointly pretested with ICR, and prepared for CATI interviewing by the ICR.

In the Main Study Phase, households that were identified as being Jewish in the screening phase were recontacted between May 8, 1990, and August 12, 1990, in an effort to complete the in-depth, detailed information requested on the Jewish character of the household, its members and related issues. Due to the considerable interview length (approximately 30 minutes), the questionnaire was divided into two parts: the "core" questionnaire and three shorter questionnaire "modules."

The core questionnaire was asked of all respondents. In addition to this core, respondents were randomly assigned to one of three groups and asked a series of more detailed questions relating to one of the following areas of inquiry (referred to as modules):

1. Jewish identity
2. Social services
3. Philanthropy

The Screening Phase had identified a total of 5,146 Jewish households over more than fifteen months of interviewing, and surveying a total of over 125,000 households. As table A.2 shows, 49 percent of these resulted in completed Phase III interviews; just over 15 percent refused to participate; and in only 13 percent of the cases was it impossible to contact any household members.

Table A.2 Results of the Main Study Phase

	Number	Percent
Nonworking	366	7.1
Nonhousehold	63	1.2
No Answer/Busy	191	3.7
Respondent no longer there	23	0.4
Answering machines	101	2.0
Refused at start	670	13.0
Refused during interview	126	2.4
Language barrier	21	0.4
Ineligible	146	2.8
Not requalified	908	17.6
Deleted/Not used interviews	25	0.5
Completed Interview	2,506	48.7
Total	5,146	100.0

The most difficult and puzzling result however, was the roughly 18 percent of respondents and/or households which failed to requalify; all of these respondents were recontacted a second time during Phase III, and all failed to validate their replies in the Screening Phase. Sections 7 and 9 contain a discussion of this group of respondents and describe how they were used in estimating the size of the Jewish population.

It was also a standard practice to attempt conversion of all refusals, so that all of this group represents "double refusals." All telephone numbers reported as "nonworking" were verified and attempts to secure new numbers were made, although this was not very successful. There was no limit on number of followup attempts, which explains the relatively low proportion of "no answer" and "busy" sample dispositions (<4%).

7. WEIGHTING PROCEDURES

7.1. Overview of Weighting Procedures

After the survey information was collected and processed, each respondent was assigned a weight. When the weights are used in tabulations of the survey data, the results automatically provide estimates of the U.S. Jewish population in each category shown in the tabulations.

The weighting method first insured that key demographic characteristics of the adult population of the total weighted sample of the 125,813 screened responding households matched the most current estimates of these demographic characteristics produced by the Census Bureau. The weighting procedure automatically adjusted for noncooperating households, as well as for those who were not at home when the interviewer telephoned and for households that did not have telephones or had multiple lines.

A second step in the weighting was carried out on the questionnaires completed in the recontact and validation phase and the main study phase of the study. This step made the weighted totals of completed questionnaires in each phase of the survey conform to the geographic and demographic profile of Jewish households at the earlier phases.

In addition, a separate weighting routine was established for each of the modules that was based on a subsample of the full set of Jewish households, so that the weighted total of each module corresponded to the full sample.

7.2. Detailed Description of Weighting

There were four stages in the preparation of the screening sample weights. First, households with more than one residential telephone number were assigned weights designed to compensate for their higher probabilities of selection—one-half for households with two telephone numbers, and one-third for households with three or more numbers. Secondly, cooperating households were poststratified, using 18 geographic strata—9 Census Divisions, and 2 categories for in or out of metropolitan areas. In the third stage, a weight was derived by poststratifying the weighted counts of the population in the sample households, using geographic-demographic strata, to the best current estimates of those strata. The strata comprised Census Region (4), age by sex (12), education of respondent (3), and race, i.e., white or other (2). The fourth stage was geographic poststratification at a state, metropolitan statistical area (MSA), or county level, depending on the size of the area. Individual counties with 75,000 or more households became individual strata. The remaining counties were grouped by individual MSAs or when necessary linked to a larger county (over 75,000 households) within the same MSA. Counties outside MSAs were grouped at the state level.

Following the weighting processes described above, the completed screener interviews were classified by their initial level of Jewish qualification and the results of the subsequent data collection efforts. During the various interviewing phases, a significant number of Jewish households that were initially considered qualified, subsequently became classified as non-Jewish. The largest proportion of these households were originally qualified because the respondents or others in the households "considered" themselves to be Jewish. Table A.3 details weighted respondents by the basis for qualification and response category in the Phase II follow-up interview.

The critical issue was how to treat the "not qualified" in estimating the total number of Jewish households. The extreme alternatives were to ignore the requalification information altogether, essentially treating the "not qualified" as refusals; or to take the additional information at "face value" and reduce the estimates of Jewish households by 789,000, to just under 3 million.

Of course, there were a wide range of options in between. To aid in the evaluation of this situation, a DJN (Distinctive Jewish Name) analysis was conducted on the respondents qualified through the screening process. The first step in this process was obtaining a reverse match for these telephone numbers; for each telephone number corresponding to a household that was listed in the white pages of any U.S. tele-

Table A.3 Qualified Jewish Households in Screener by Reporting Status in Validation Interview

	Basis of qualification in screener				
Reporting status of later interviews	*Total*	*Religion*	*Consider*	*Raised*	*Parents*
Known Jewish households	1,896,000	1,167,000	460,000	80,000	189,000
	100.0%	61.6	24.2	4.2	9.9
Refused Phase III	506,000	242,000	176,000	29,000	59,000
	100.0%	47.9	34.8	5.8	11.6
Other nonresponse	563,000	200,000	246,000	29,000	88,000
	100.0%	35.4	43.8	5.1	15.7
Non qualified	789,000	128,000	466,000	57,000	138,000
	100.0%	16.2	59.0	7.2	17.5
Total	3,753,000	1,737,000	1,347,000	195,000	474,000
	100.0	46.3	35.9	5.2	12.6

phone directory, the name and address of the subscriber was obtained. The surnames were then matched against a data file of distinctive Jewish surnames provided by the NTAC. The results are shown in table A.4.

As is evident from table A.4, the Not Qualified segment exhibits strikingly different proportions of DJN's from the other groups. Based on this and related information, the determination was made that all respondents originally qualified on the basis of Religion were most likely Refusals, and should remains as qualified Jewish households; conversely, among the other groups, the unweighted ratios of DJN's indicated a likely true qualification rate of 17.5 percent.

Based on these assessments, the estimated Jewish households were adjusted to those shown in table A.5. The impact of these adjustments were to reduce the estimates of Jewish households from 3.753 million to 3.208 million, a reduction of about 14.5 percent.

Table A.4 Percentage of Sample with Distinctive Jewish Surnames (Base = Qualifiers with a Located Surname)

	Basis of qualification in screener				
Reporting status in later interviews	*Total*	*Religion*	*Consider*	*Raised*	*Parents*
Known Jewish household	16.7	23.3	5.6	10.5	4.8
Refused Phase III	13.8	20.0	8.0	9.5	7.8
Other nonresponse	10.9	21.2	4.9	6.7	3.8
Not qualified	2.6	8.6	1.5	0.0	1.6

Table A.5 Final Estimates of Jewish Households Reflecting Adjustments to "Not Qualified" Call Results

	Basis of qualification in Screener				
Reporting status in later interviews	*Total*	*Religion*	*Consider*	*Raised*	*Parents*
Known Jewish HH	1,896,000	1,167,000	460,000	80,000	189,000
	100.0%	61.6	24.2	4.2	9.9
Refused Phase III	506,000	242,000	176,000	29,000	59,000
	100.0%	47.9	34.8	5.8	11.6
Other Nonresponse	563,000	200,000	246,000	29,000	88,000
	100.0%	35.4	43.8	5.1	15.7
Not Qualified	244,000	128,000	82,000	10,000	24,000
	100.0%	52.4	33.6	4.1	9.9
Total	3,208,000	1,737,000	963,000	148,000	360,000
	100.0%	54.1	30.0	4.6	11.2

The adjustments to the weighted estimates of Jewish households in table A.5 required a two-phase adjustment to the weighted dataset:

1. The indicated proportions of Not Qualified respondents needed to be weighted downward to the indicated totals, while non-Jewish households required a compensatory weight to maintain Total Household in the entire Screening Sample.
2. The completed Phase III interviews were then weighted to the estimates of Total Jewish Households, for analyses based on Jewish households only.

The first step was accomplished by stratifying based on Census Division, and within Division, by (1) non-Jewish Qualifiers; (2) Households qualified in the screener as Jewish based on other than Religion, who became "not Qualified in Phase III; and, (3) all other Jewish households. The second group represents those respondents whose estimate of Jewish affiliation was to be adjusted in this process. The revised weights were substituted in the individual data records, completing reconciliation of the full Screener Data set.

The procedure described above was carried out for the full sample and is therefore applicable to the core questionnaire that was administered to all sample households. However, each sample data record also includes a module weight in addition to the household and population weights for the core questions. The weighting procedure for the modules duplicated that of the previous section: a poststratification scheme incorporating census region and level of Jewish qualification. A simple expansion factor, to weight each module's sample total in each cell was computed, multiplied by the household weight, and incorporated into the sample record.

Separate population weights were also developed for the statistics obtained from the randomly selected adult in each household. Essentially, these weights incorporated the household weights multiplied by the number of adults in the sample households.

8. APPLICATION OF WEIGHTS

Given the character and complexity of the survey instrument itself, a determination as to which of the weights described above to utilize for a particular statistic is not always apparent. The following explanation and examples should help in eliminating uncertainties.

Household weights should be used for developing estimates in the following types of situations:

1. Where the analysis, table, or distribution being produced is clearly based on household demographics. Examples include:

   - The number of households by level of Jewish qualification;
   - Distributions of households by number of children, number of adults, number of Jewish adults, age of oldest member, or household income distributions.
   - Household distributions based on qualification of one or more members; such as "are you or any member of your household currently a member of a synagogue or temple?"

2. Where the analysis or distribution utilizes variables constructed from the roster of household members. Examples include:

   - Age or educational attainment of all household members or subsets of all members.
   - Country of origin, or employment status, of all household members or adult household members.

The populations weights are applicable only in those situations where the respondent answers to a specific question about himself or herself, and are to be utilized to represent all adult members in Jewish households. For example:

- Opinions about various public issues.
- Distributions of Jewish religious denomination, or Jewish ethnicity.
- Personal attendance at Jewish religious services.

In certain rare situations users may need to devise their own weighting schemes to establish a fully weighted sample base. This is most likely to occur when the adult members of a sample household exceed the number for which data was requested. For example, detailed information as to marital status was requested for only four members 18 years of age and older. If a particular sample household had five members, there are a number of options depending upon one's objectives and the characteristics of the household:

- A balance line of "not-reported" could be incorporated into the tables being produced.

- The simplest weighting method would be to weight each of the four responses by 1.25 in addition to application of the household weight. Depending, however, upon the characteristics of the member for whom no data is available, alternative approaches might prove more desirable.
- If the missing number's data represented one of three adult children, a better approach might be to weight the data for the two children for which data is present by 1.5, while keeping the parent's weight at 1.0.
- Alternatively, one could compensate for the missing member information on an overall basis. For example, one could categorize all qualified members by age, sex, region, etc., using the household weights; categorize those for which data was reported in a similar matrix using the household weight; and finally computing a weight for each cell which would increase the base of those responding to the weighted total in the first matrix.

In most cases, the bias created by simply ignoring the small discrepancies will be minimal. However, the user needs to make these decisions on a case-by-case basis, possibly trying alternative methods and comparing the results.

Finally, the module weights should obviously be used for tabulations of items in any of the modules regardless of whether simple totals of module items are tabulated or there are cross-classifications with other nonmodule items.

9. ACCURACY OF DATA

9.1. Nonsampling Errors

All population surveys are subject to the possibility of errors arising from sampling, nonresponse, and respondents providing the wrong information, and the NJPS is no exception. The response rate to identify potential Jewish households was approximately 50 percent. This Is lower than most surveys that make efforts to insure high quality strive to achieve. (The low response rate was partially caused by the contractor's need for each set of sample cases assigned for interview to be completed in a few days. This made intensive followup in the screener impractical.) The concern over the effect of nonresponse on the statistics is not so much on the size of the nonresponse since this is adjusted for in the weighting, but on the likelihood that nonrespondents are somewhat different from respondents. Although variations in response rates by geography, age, sex, race, and educational attainment were adjusted for in the weighting, there was still the possibility that Jews and non-Jews responded at different rates.

To test whether this occurred at an important level, the telephone numbers of approximately 10,000 completed interviews and for about 10,000 nonrespondents were matched against telephone listings to obtain the household names, and the percentage of each group having distinctive Jewish names was calculated. The percentage for the completed cases was 1.38 percent and for the nonrespondents was 1.29. The difference between the two is well within the bounds of sampling error. Although distinctive Jewish names account for a minority of all Jews, this test does provide support for the view that nonresponse did not have an important impact on the reliability of the count of the Jewish population.

In regard to errors in reporting whether a person is Jewish, previous studies indicate that the errors are in the direction of understating the count of the Jewish population, although the size of the understatement does not seem to be very large. A particular concern in the NJPS was the fairly large number of cases where respondents in households reporting the presence of one or more Jews in the screening operation, reversed themselves in the detailed interview. Of all households reported as having Jews in the screener, 18 percent were reported as nonqualified in the detailed interview. There was a possibility that this was a hidden form of refusal, rather than errors in the original classification of the households or changes in household membership.

A test similar to the one on refusals was carried out for the nonqualified households. The telephone numbers for the 5,146 households were reported as Jewish in the screening interview were matched against telephone listings, and those with distinctive Jewish names (DJN) were identified. The detailed results of the match are reported in Section 7. They can be summarized as follows: In households that reported themselves as Jewish in the detailed interviews, 16.8 percent had DJN's. The rates were slightly smaller for refusals (13.9 percent) and for those who could not be contacted (10.9 percent). However, the percentage was only 2.9 percent for households who were reported as not Jewish in the detailed interview. It is, of course, possible that DJN households are less reticent than others in acknowledging to a telephone interviewer the fact that all or some of the household members are Jewish, but the evidence is that underreporting did occur, but not to a very serious extent. An adjustment in the weights of about 8 percent was made to account for the unreported Jews in the estimates of the total number of Jews. Since questionnaire information was not obtained for them, the statistics on characteristics of Jews may be subject to small biases if the Jewish nonqualifiers are very different from those who responded.

As mentioned earlier, other studies have reported that there is some understatement of reporting of Jewish heritage in interviews surveys. No adjustments were made for such possible understatement since firm data on its size does not exist. As a result, the estimate of the size of the Jewish population is probably somewhat on the low side.

It is not possible to quantify the effects of the relatively high nonresponse rates, the possibility that some respondents might have deliberately misreported their religious affiliations, errors arising from misunderstanding of the questions, or other problems in the data. As indicated above, the test done with the presence of Distinctive Jewish Names did not detect any important problems. Furthermore, comparisons of the estimates of total Jewish population with the results of local area surveys carried out in or near 1990, did not show any important discrepancies. The screener questionnaire that inquired about Jewish affiliations also identified other major U.S. religious groupings, and estimates of their membership corresponded reasonably well with independent estimates of the membership.

Consequently, all of the tests we were able to carry out failed to turn up any major problems in the data. However, it seems reasonable to assume that persons who did not respond are somewhat different from respondents, and the other potential sources of error must also have had some impact. When comparisons are made, either over time, or among subgroups of Jewish persons (e.g., between those with a relatively high level of Jewish education and others, persons with synagogue affiliation and unaffiliated, etc.), it would be prudent to avoid analyses or explanations of small differences, even if they are statistically significant. However, the evidence is that large and important differences do reflect real phenomena, and can be relied on.

9.2. Sampling Variability

Sample surveys are subject to sampling error arising from the fact that the results may differ from what would have been obtained if the whole population had been interviewed. The size of the sampling error of an estimate depends on the number of interviews and the sample design. For estimates of the number of Jewish households, the sample size is 125,813 screened households. The screened sample was virtually a simple random sample. As a result, it is very likely (the chances are about 95 percent) that the number of Jewish households is within a range plus or minus 3 percent around the estimate shown in this report. For estimates of the Jewish population, the range is slightly higher since sampling variability, will affect both the estimate of the number of Jewish households and of the average number of Jews in those households. The 95 percent range is plus or minus 3.5 percent. These ranges are the limits within which the results of repeated sampling in the same time period could be expected to vary 95 percent of the time, assuming the same sampling procedure, the same interviewers, and the same questionnaire.

Unfortunately, due to the complex nature of the sample design and weighting method used in estimating the characteristics of the Jewish population, it is not possible to give a simple formula that will provide estimates of the standard errors for all types of estimates. To begin with, there are three basic samples embedded in the survey:

1. The household sample can be considered as the equivalent of a simple random sample of 2,441 households.
2. For population statistics based on data reported for all household members, the sample size is 6,514. However, for most estimates of this type, the standard errors will be greater than what would be achieved with a simple random sample of 6,514 because of the presence of intra-class correlation, that is the tendency of household members to be more alike than would be the case of persons chosen at random. The intra-class correlation introduces a design effect that should be superimposed on the simple formula for the standard error.
3. Population statistics based on data reported for only one household member, selected at random, are also based on a sample size of 2,441. However, since the chance of selection of any person depends on the number of adults in the household the sample is not equivalent to a simple random sample of 2,441. The varying probabilities of selection also create a design effect.

The standard error of an estimate of a percentage can be approximated by:

$$\sqrt{D.p.(1-p)/Rn}$$

where p is the estimated percentage, D is the design effect, R is the proportion of Jews in the segment for which percentages are computed, and n is the sample size, that is 2,441 or 6,514. When percentages are computed of all Jewish households or persons, R is equal to 1; when the base of the percentage is a subgroup of all households or persons (e.g., households observing certain rituals, all females, persons in a particular group), the value of R is the fraction of all households or persons in that subgroup.

The value of D is 1 for household statistics. For population statistics, the value will depend on the item being estimated. Although it is possible to calculate an estimate of the value of D for each item (or alternatively, a relatively unbiased estimate of the standard error), we assume most analysts will not want to make the fairly extensive effort needed for such calculations. Guidelines for approximating D follow.

- As stated earlier, D can be considered equal to one for household statistics.
- For items based on data reported for all household members, D will be in the range 1 to 2.7. It will be close to 1 for percentages based on a subset of the Jewish population (e.g., adult males, currently widowed persons, persons born abroad, disabled, etc.) At the other extreme, the value will be close to 2.7 on items for which household members are likely to have similar characteristics (e.g., the percentage of Jews who belong to conservative congregations). The 2.7 is the average size of Jewish households, and when D has this value, the effect on the standard error is to treat the statistic as a household item with a sample size of 2,441 rather than a population item. For other types of percentages, the value of D will be somewhere in the 1 to 2.7 range; the more alike members of a household are likely to be, the greater should be the value of D used in the calculations.
- The value of D is about 1.2 for items based on data reported for only one adult in the household. This design effect reflects the effect on sampling errors of having varying probabilities of selection, depending on the household size. For example, adults living in one-adult households will have twice the chance of selection as those in two-adult households, three times the chance as those in households containing three adults, etc.

It should also be noted that the value of n is lower for items in the modules asked for a subsample of respondents than for other items. Since the modules are based on a one-third subsample, the sample size of 2,441 and 6,514 are reduced to 814 and 2,171. When the sample sizes used in the base of percentages are obtained by simply counting the number of records used in the calculations, the count automatically provides the value of R, and it is unnecessary to calculate R, or to be concerned over whether or not the item is one of the modules.

NOTES

1. This is not a serious problem since only a few households had four children—1.5 percent of the households in NJPS had four children under age 18.

2. Demography can be defined as the statistical study of a population group and its size, density, distribution, and vital statistics (birth, marriage, divorce, and death).

3. In utilizing data attributed to different numbers of responses, the results might not always be consistent across tables. For example, if we were to measure the total number of children by age and gender and then measure the total number of children by region the results might be slightly different. These minor discrepancies may be due to missing cases, unanswered questions, uncategorized responses, and the differing cell sizes, which may result in different computer-based projections of the weighted data. Also, the tallying of rounded scores may produce different totals than if the statistics had not been rounded.

4. We note that such syncretic forms of Judaism are unacceptable to the Jewish tradition and to communal organizations, so these children have been excluded from the Core Jewish population category. We can assume that the majority of children being raised in other religions are the product of interfaith marriages, though some may be through conversion. There appear to be several thousand households nationally that contain Jewish children but no Jewish adults. This arises when an intermarriage results in the non-Jewish spouse maintaining custody of the child(ren) after divorce from the Jewish spouse, where the divorce settlement stipulates the child be raised as a Jew, or the Jewish spouse dies.

5. The choice of the youngest child was necessitated by the fact that for parents of teenagers, the eldest child was often an adult for whom we lacked data. We also note that some parents, particularly those who are younger, may not have yet completed their fertility.

6. This is apart from the goal of maximizing the child's own welfare. In our research, both questions will be reviewed.

7. Since over 95 percent of Core Jewish adults in NJPS self-identified as white, we provide the comparison with white children nationwide. This is due to the strong relationship between household composition and race in American society.

8. Per capita income refers to the household income divided by the number of persons in the household. This measurement reflects more accurately the real economic level of individuals.

9. According to our data, about 400,000 children are currently enrolled in Jewish education, one-third of them in full-time day schools or Yeshivoth.

10. 200,000 of the 306,000 JNR children, nearly two-thirds, are children of intermarriage.

11. This is a life cycle stage that is reached at different ages between 25 and 45 in contemporary American society.

12. We note the slight discrepancy with the 1990 CJF *Highlights,* which estimated that 28 percent of children living in mixed households were being raised Jewish. Our unweighted figure of 30 percent is based on a subsample of two-parent households.

13. A preliminary version of this study, "Religious Socialization of Children of Interfaith Couples: The Role of Parents' Background Differences—A Case Study of Jews Married to Non-Jews," by Ariela Keysar, Egon Mayer and Barry A. Kosmin, was published in the 1993 American Statistical Association Winter Conference's proceedings.

14. The CHAID method partitions a contingency table produced from cross-tabulation of three or more variables by using a semi-hierarchical, sequential procedure. The procedure is semi-hierarchical in the sense that it determines the smallest number of groupings (splits) of the levels of a predictor by means of a process of pairwise merging (and then separating) of the response levels on each of the predictors. Once the number of splits (categories) for each predictor has been determined in the semi-hierarchical process, the original sample is split on the basis of the most significant predictor. The analysis is sequential in the sense that each of the subgroups of the sample produced by that split is then treated as a new "parent group" (candidate for splitting) and is split in the same fashion until any possible remaining split of a group is not significant, or until the size of a group is too small to provide meaningful probability estimates (Perreault and Barksdale 1980). The rules we imposed for the running of the CHAID procedure are a minimum cell size of five cases and a critical p-value of 0.05.

15. JR=Jew by religion; JN=Jew with no religion; GN=Gentile with no religion; CH=Christian. In this case, the first half of the identifier refers to the mother's religion status; the second half, to the father's.

16. In this case, the first half of the identifier refers to the father and the second half to the mother.

17. The New York questionnaire addressed the question on Jewish education to the respondent only, while the national study asked about the other adults in the household as well.

18. When we compare children rather than households, a different procedure is applied that does not allow a test of significance. However, in Table 5.5 the gap between the two subpopulations is large enough for us to claim that they are substantial.

19. Due to the small number of exogamous Orthodox families we combine Orthodox and Conservative exogamous families.

20. By focal child we mean one child from each household representing the universe of Jewish children.

21. The NSFH was carried out in 1987 and 1988 by the Center For Demography and Ecology and the Department of Sociology of the University of Wisconsin-Madison. The survey included a main sample of 9,643 respondents representative of the noninstitutionalized United States population age 19 and older.

22. There may have been additional cases of households with adopted children. The NJPS questionnaire requested this information only of households with a female member between the ages of 18 and 44. Other household types—women or couples age 45 and over, as well as single male households—may also have contained adopted children.

23. This includes both two-parent and single-parent families.

24. We realize that there could be switches from one category to another, as some of the single women marry non-Jews, others divorce and marry in or out—choosing a spouse of a different religion than their current spouse. There could also be remarriages that are most likely to be intermarriages. All these patterns will alter the number of women in the two categories. For the sake of simplicity in the first projection, these patterns are ignored.

25. Total fertility rate represents the overall number of children a woman has during her childbearing years.

26. This is based on the U.S. white population in 1990.

27. Namely, we maintain current intermarriage rates among married women and do not allow further investigation among unmarried women or men.

28. Seven percent are in miscellaneous Jewish denominations.

29. Joseph Waksberg is an internationally known expert in the area of social research, sampling methods, study design and analysis.

WORKS CITED

Ackerman, Walter I. 1986. "New Models of Jewish Education: The Bureau Community Perspective." *Jewish Education* 54, no. 2 (Summer): 3–8.

Adelson, Joseph. 1980. *Handbook of Adolescent Psychology.* New York: John Whiley and Sons.

Ain, Meryl. 1993. "Teens Warming to Spending Summer in Israel." *New York Jewish Week,* October 20.

Alba, Richard. 1990. *Ethnic Identity: The Transformation of White America.* New Haven: Yale University Press.

Allport, Gordon. 1995. *Becoming: Basic Considerations for a Psychology of Personality.* New Haven: Yale University Press.

Amato, P. R. and B. Keith. 1991. "Separation from a Parent during Childhood and Adult Socio-Economic Attachment." *Social Forces.* 70:187–206.

Anderson, A. A. and W. M. Fleming. 1986. "Late Adolescents' Home Leaving Strategies: Predicting Ego Identity and College Adjustment." *Adolescence* 11, no. 82:453–459.

————. 1986. "Late Adolescents' Identity Formation: Individuation from the Family of Origin." *Adolescence* 11, no. 84:785–795.

Arnow, David. 1994. "Toward a Psychology of Jewish Identity: A Multi-Dimensional Approach." *Journal of Jewish Communal Service* 71, no. 1:29–36.

Association of Jewish Family and Children's Agencies Survey on Adoption Services. 1993. *Jewish Family Service Agencies* (June).

Bennett, J. W. 1969. *Northern Plainsmen: Adaptive Strategy and Agricultural Life.* Arlington Heights, Ill.: AHM Publishers.

Berger, Gabriel. 1988. "Jewish Child Care: A Challenge and Opportunity." In *Research Report #3.* Waltham, Mass.: Cohen Center, Brandeis University.

B'nai B'rith Hillel Foundations Center for Campus Study and the Cohen Center for Modern Jewish Studies at Brandeis University. 1990. "A Profile of Hillel Leaders" (August).

Borman, Kathryn. 1982. *The Social Life of Children in a Changing Society.* Hillsdale, N.J.: Lawrence Erlbaum Associates Publishers.

Campbell, Susan B., and Patricia Cluss. 1982. "Peer Relationships of Young Children with Behavior Problems." In *Peer Relationships and Social Skills in Children,* edited by Rubin and Ross. New York: Springer Verlag.

Center for Demography and Ecology and the Department of Sociology of the University of Wisconsin-Madison. 1988. *The National Survey of Family and Households.*

Chadwick, Bruce, and Tim Heaton. 1992. *Statistical Handbook on the American Family,* Phoenix, Ariz.: Onyx Press.

Chazan, Barry. 1997. *Does the Teen Israel Experience Make a Difference?* New York: Israel Experience Inc.

Cherlin, Andrew, and Carin Celebuski. 1982. "Are Jewish Families Different?" *American Jewish Committee.* New York: American Jewish Committee.

Chiswick, Barry. 1993. "Working and Family Life: The Experiences of Jewish Women in America." Paper presented at University of Illinois at Chicago, October.

Chiswick, Carmel. 1994. "The Economic Environment of American Jewry." Paper presented at University of Illinois at Chicago, February.

Cohen, Sarale. 1978. "Maternal Employment and Mother-Child Interaction." *Merrill Palmer Quarterly* (July): 189–197.

Cohen, Steven. 1995. "The Impact of Varieties of Jewish Education Upon Jewish Identity: An Inter-Generational Perspective." *Contemporary Jewry* 68–96.

Coleman, James 1974. *Youth Transition to Adulthood.* Chicago: University of Chicago Press.

———. 1993. "The Rational Reconstruction of Society." *American Sociological Review* 58:1–15.

Cornwall, M. 1988. "The Influence of Three Agents of Socialization." In *The Religion and Family Connection,* edited by D. L. Thomas, vol. 16 Provo, Utah: Brigham Young University.

Dash-Moore, Deborah. 1981. *At Home in America: Second-Generation New York Jews.* New York: Columbia University Press.

———. 1994. *To the Golden Cities: Pursuing the American Jewish Dream in Miami and L.A.* New York: Free Press.

Dashefsky, Arnold, and Howard Shapiro. 1974. *Ethnic Identification among American Jews.* Lexington, Mass.: Heathland Company.

DeAnda, Diane. 1986. "Adolescents. " *The Social Work Encyclopedia.* Silver Spring, Md.: National Association of Social Workers.

DellaPergola, Sergio. 1991. "New Data on Demography and Identification among Jews in the United States." *Contemporary Jewry* 12:67–98.

Dudley, Roger L., and Margaret G. Dudley. 1986. "Transmission of Religious Values from Parents to Adolescents." *Review of Religious Research* 28, no. 1. (September): 3–15.

Dunn, Judy. 1986. "Growing Up in a Family World: Issues in the Study of Social Development in Young Children." In *Children of Social Worlds: Development in a Social Context.* Edited by Richards and Light. Cambridge, Mass.: Harvard University Press.

Edelman, Alan. 1993. "Why Should I Send My Child to Visit Israel?" *Kansas City Jewish Chronicle,* 19, November 4.

Eisenstadt, S. N. 1956. *From Generation to Generation: Age Groups and Social Structure.* New York: The Cromwell-Collier Publishing Company.

Elkin, Frederick, and Gerald Handel. 1984. *The Child Society: The Process of Socialization.* New York: Random House.

Erikson, Erik. 1968. *Identity, Youth and Crisis.* New York: W. W. Norton and Company.

———. 1977. *Childhood and Society.* New York: W. W. Norton and Company.

———. 1980. *Identity and the Life Cycle.* New York: W. W. Norton and Company.

———. 1997. *The Life Cycle Completed.* New York: W. W. Norton and Company.

Erickson, Joseph. 1992. "Adolescent Religious Development and Commitment: A Structural Equation Model of the Role of Family, Peer Group and Educational Influences." *Journal for the Scientific Study of Religion.* 31, no. 2, (June) 131–152.

Finkel, Norman. 1985. "The Development of Day Care under Jewish Auspices." *Journal of Jewish Communal Service* 62, no. 2 (Winter): 170–177.

Fishkoff, Sue. 1993. "The Cost of Living as a Jew." *The Jerusalem Post,* 11 September.

Fishman, Sylvia Barack, and Alice Goldstein. 1993. *When They Are Grown Will They Not De-*

part: Jewish Education and Jewish Behavior of American Adults. Waltham, Mass.: Cohen Center for Modern Jewish Studies, Brandeis University.

Flavell, J. H. 1985. *Cognitive Development.* Englewood, N.J.: Prentice Hall.

Friedman, Norman. 1984. "On the 'Non-Effects' of Jewish Education on Most Students: A Critique." *Jewish Education* 52, no. 2 (Summer): 30–33.

Friedman, Peter, and Mark Zober. 1987. "Factors Influencing Synagogue Affiliation: A Multi-Community Analysis." In *Building an Awareness of a Continental Jewish Community—North American Jewish Data Bank Occasional Paper no. 3.* New York: North American Jewish Data Bank.

Ganapol, Alan. 1993. *Young Judea Continuity Study.* New York: Marketquest.

Gerth, Hans, and C. Wright Mills. 1953. *Character and Social Structure: The Psychology of Social Institutions.* New York: Harcourt, Brace and World.

Glazer, Nathan. 1990. "American Jewry or American Judaism." *Society* 28:14–20.

Gold, Michael. 1986. "Adoption as an Option." *B'nai B'rith Jewish Monthly,* June–July, 18–22.

———. 1988. *And Hannah Wept.* Philadelphia: Jewish Publication Society.

Goldscheider, Calvin. 1993. "A Century of Jewish Fertility in an American Community: Cohort Trends and Differentials." In *Papers in Jewish Demography,* edited by Uziel O. Schmelz and Sergio DellaPergola. Jerusalem: The Hebrew University of Jerusalem—The Auraham Herman Institute of Contemporary Jewry 129–144.

Goldscheider, Calvin, and Frances K. Goldscheider. 1993. "Transition to Jewish Adulthood: Education, Marriage and Fertility." In *Papers in Jewish Demography,* edited by Uziel O. Schmelz and Sergio DellaPergola. Jerusalem: The Hebrew University of Jerusalem—The Auraham Herman Institute of Contemporary Jewry 129–144.

Goldstein, Alice, and Sylvia Barack Fishman. 1993. *Teach Your Children When They Are Young: Contemporary Jewish Education in the United States.* Waltham, Mass.: Cohen Center for Modern Jewish Studies, Brandeis University.

Goldstein, Sidney. 1992. "Profile of American Jewry: Insights from the 1990 National Jewish Population Survey." *American Jewish Yearbook.* New York: American Jewish Committee.

———. 1992. "The Demographics of American Jewry." In *World Jewish Population Trends and Policies,* edited by Sergio DellaPergola and Leah Cohen. Jerusalem: Graph Press, 53–84.

Goldstein, Sidney, and Alice Goldstein. 1996. *Jews on the Move: Implications for Jewish Identity.* Albany, N.Y.: State Uuniversity of New York Press.

Harter, S. 1983. "Developmental Perspectives on the Self System." In *Handbook of Child Psychology: Socialization, Personality and Social Development.* edited by E. M. Hetherington. Vol. 4. New York: Wiley Publishing Company.

Herman, Simon N. 1970. *Israelis and Jews: The Continuity of an Identity.* New York: Random House.

———. 1977. *Jewish Identity: A Social and Psychological Perspective.* New Brunswick, N.J.: Transaction Publishers.

Hernandez, Donald. 1993. *America's Children: Resources from Family, Government and the Economy.* New York: Russel Sage Foundation.

Hetherington, E. M., and W. N. Morris. 1978. "The Family and Primary Groups." In *Introductory Psychology in Depth: Developmental Topics,* edited by W. H. Holtzman. New York: Harper and Row.

Himmelfarb, Harold. 1982. "Research on American Jewish Identity and Identification:

Progress, Pitfalls and Progress." In *Understanding American Jewry.* New Brunswick, N.J.: Transaction Books.

Hoenig, Barbara. 1991. "Briefing Paper on Intermarriage." Paper presented at Council of Jewish Federations, New York, December.

Hoffman, Lois Wladis. 1989. "Effects of Maternal Employment in the Two-Parent Family." *American Psychologist* 44, no. 2 (February): 283–292.

Hoge, Dean, Gregory Petrillo, and Ella Smith. 1982. "Transmission of Religious and Social Values from Parents to Teenage Children." *Journal of Marriage and the Family* 44, no. 3 (August): 569–579.

Horowitz, Bethamie, and Jeffrey Solomon. 1992. "Why is this City Different from all Other Cities? New York and the National Jewish Population Survey. 1991." *Journal of Jewish Communal Service.* New York. Volume 68, no. 4.

Horowitz, Bethamie. 1993. *The 1991 New York Jewish Population Study.* New York: UJA-Federation.

Huberman, Steve. 1993. "Preparing for the Jewish Future" In *Reconstructionist* (April): 13–16.

Jewish Education Service of North America. 1993. "Research Report." (December). New York: Jewish Education Service of North America.

———. 1995. "Planning for Jewish Continuity: Synagogue-Federation Collaboration." (November). New York: Jewish Education Service of North America.

Jewish Family Services of Baltimore. 1993. "Infertility and the Jewish Community." Baltimore, Md.: Jewish Family Services of Baltimore.

Josselyn, Irene. 1967. *The Adolescent and His World.* New York: Family Association Service of America.

Kagen, Ed. 1994. *JCCs and Jewish Identity—Confirming the Connection.* New York: JCC Association Research Center.

Kahane, Reuven. 1975. "Informal Youth Organizations: A General Model." *Sociological Inquiry* 45, no. 4:17–28.

Kallen, Evelyn. 1977. *Spanning the Generations: A Study of Jewish Identity.* Toronto: Longman Canada.

Kaplan, Aryeh. 1980. *The Living Torah.* New York: Maznain Publishing Corporation.

Keysar, Ariela, Egon Mayer, and Barry Kosmin. 1993. *Religious Socialization of Children of Interfaith Couples: The Role of Parents' Background Differences—A Case Study of Jews Married to Non-Jews.* New York: American Statistical Association Winter Conference Proceedings.

Keysar, Ariela. 1994. "Single-Parent Families' Participation in the Jewish Community." *Journal of Jewish Communal Service* (Winter/Spring): 70, nos. 2/3:127–133.

Keysar, Ariela, and Barry Kosmin. 1995. "The Impact of Religious Identification on Differences in Educational Attainment among American Women in 1990." *Journal for the Scientific Study of Religion.* 34, no. 1, (March.): 49–62.

Knudten, Richard. 1967. *The Sociology of Religion: An Anthology.* New York: Appelton Century Crofts.

Kosmin, Barry A., and Seymour P. Lachman. 1993. *One Nation under God: Religion in Contemporary American Society.* New York: Harmony.

Kosmin, Barry A, Sidney Goldstein, Joseph Waksberg, Nava Lerer, Ariela Keysar, and Jeffrey

Scheckner. 1991. *Highlights of the CJF 1990 National Jewish Population Survey.* New York: Council of Jewish Federations.

Lamott, Ann. 1993. "When Going It Alone Turns Out To Be Not So Alone At All" *The New York Times,* 12, August C-9.

Lazerwitz, Bernard. 1953. "Some Factors in Jewish Identity." *Jewish Social Studies* (January) 15: 3–24.

Liebman, A. 1978. *Jews and the Left.* New York: Wiley and Sons.

Lipset, Seymour Martin. 1994. *The Power of Jewish Education.* Los Angeles: Wilstein Institute of Jewish Policy Studies.

Lipsitz, Gail. 1995. "Adoption and the Jewish Family," *Adoptive Families,* Spring, 32–33, 37.

Lipsitz, Gail, and Irene Jordan. 1993. "Parenting: Not Just Kid Stuff." *Baltimore Jewish Times,* 26, November 42–43.

Lipsitz, Gail, Lucy Steinitz, Myra Hettleman, and Irene Jordan. 1991. "Cross-Cultural Adoption: New Horizons for Jewish Family and Service Agencies." *Journal of Jewish Communal Service* (Spring):

London, Aaron. 1993. "Reform Youth Convention Confronts Continuity." *American Israelite,* 19 August, B7, B16.

London, Perry. 1990. "Jewish Identity Formation in the Family: A Taste of Honey." Pamphlet. Los Angeles: University of Judaism.

Lubeck, Sally, and Patricia Garrett. 1988. "Child Care 2000: Policy Options for the Future." *Social Policy* 67, no. 3 (Spring): 222–227.

Martin, William, and Celia Stendler. 1959. *Child Behavior and Development.* New York: Harcourt, Brace and World.

Marx, Fern. 1985. "Child Care." In Harriette and John McAdoo. *Services to Young Families* by American Public Welfare Association.

Marx, Karl. 1964. *Selected Writings in Sociology and Social Philosophy.* New York: McGraw Hill.

Mayer, Egon. 1994. "Will the Grandchildren of Intermarriage be Jews? The Chances are Greater than You Think." *Moment* 19, no. 2 (April): 50–53, 78.

Mead, George H. 1934. *Mind, Self and Society From the Standpoint of a Social Behaviorist.* Chicago: University of Chicago Press.

Medding, Peter, Gary Tobin, Sylvia Barack Fishman, and Modechai Rimor. 1992. "Jewish Identity in Conversionary and Mixed Marriages." *American Jewish Year Book* edited by David Singer. New York: American Jewish Committee.

Miller, D. R. 1963. "The Study of Social Relationships: Situation and Identity and Sound Interaction." In *Psychology: A Study of Science.* Vol. 5. edited by S. Kerch. New York: McGraw Hill.

Mittelberg, David. 1994. *The Israel Visit and Jewish Identification.* New York: Institute on American Jewish-Israeli Relations, the American Jewish Committee.

Mott, Frank, and Joyce Abma. 1992. "Contemporary Jewish Fertility: Does Religion Make a Difference?" *Contemporary Jewry* 13: 74–94.

———. 1993. "Intermarriage, Childbearing and Intergenerational Transmission of Jewish Identity: Prospects for the Future of American Jewry." Paper presented at a meeting of the Society for Research on Social Problems, Miami, August.

National Center for Health Statistics Document HE20. 6217 Item 0508-B, 1991. *Advance An-*

nual Report on Final 1989–90 Divorce Data. Washington, D.C.: National Center for Health Statistics.

North American Commission on Jewish Identity and Continuity. 1995. "To Renew and Sanctify: A Call to Action." Report of the North American Commission on Jewish Identity and Continuity. New York: Council of Jewish Federations.

Ogbu, J. U. 1979. "Social Stratification and the Socialization of Confidence." *Anthropology and Education Quarterly* 10: 10–14.

———. 1982. "Socialization : A Cultural Ecological Approach." In *The Social Life of Children in a Changing Society,* edited by Kathryn M. Borman. Hillsdale, N.J.: Lawrence Erlbaum Associates Publishers.

Olson, G. M. 1981. "The Cognition of Specific Persons." In Lamb and Sherrod, eds., *Infant Social Cognition: Empirical and Theoretical Considerations.* Hillsdale, N.J.: Lawrence Erlbaum Associates.

Openshaw, D. Kim, Darwin L. Thomas, and Boyd C. Rollins. 1983. "Socialization and Adolescent Self-Esteem: Symbolic Interaction and Social Learning Explanations" *Adolescence* 18, no. 70 (Summer): 317–325.

Ozorak, Elizabeth Weiss. 1989. "Social and Cognitive Influences on the Development of Religious Beliefs and Commitment in Adolescence." *Journal for the Scientific Study of Religion* 28, no. 4 (December): 448–463.

Parker, Mitchell, and Eugene Gaier. 1980. "Religion, Religious Beliefs, and Religious Practices among Conservative Jewish Adolescents." *Adolescence* XVI: 361–374.

Pepper, Sarah K. 1995. *Jewish Intermarriage as Related to Fertility: A Relevant Concern for Survival.* Unpublished.

Perreault, W. D., and H. C. Barksdale. 1980. "A Model-free Approach for Analysis of Complex Contingency Data in Survey Research." *Journal of Marketing Research* 17: 503–515.

Perry, D. G., and L. C. Perry. 1983. "Social Learning, Causal Attribution and Moral Internalization." In *Learning in Children: Progress in Cognitive Development Research,* edited by J. Bisanz, G. L. Bisanz & R. V. Krail, Jr. New York: Springer-Verlag.

Phillips, Bruce. 1997. *Reexamining Intermarriage: Trends, Textures and Strategies.* Boston and New York: American Jewish Committee and the Wilstein Institute.

Piaget, J., and B. Inhelder. 1958. *The Growth of Logical Thinking from Childhood to Adolescence.* New York: Basic Books.

Rapoport, Tamar. 1989. "Experimentation and Control: A Conceptual Framework for the Comparative Analysis of Socialization Agencies." *Human Relations* 42: no. 11: 957–973.

Rapoport, Tamar, and Reuven Kahane. 1988. "Informal Socialization Agencies and Role Development." *Sociological Inquiry* 58, no. 1, 49–74.

Reeves, Diane L. 1992. *The Child Care Crisis.* Santa Barbara, Calif.: ABC-CLIO.

Richards, Leslie, and Cynthia Schmiege. 1993. "Problems, and Strengths of Single-Parent Families: Implications for Practice and Policy." *Family Relations* 43, no. 3 (July) 277–285.

Richards, Martin, and Paul Light. 1986. *Children of Social Worlds: Development in a Social Context.* Cambridge: Harvard University Press.

Ritterband, Paul. 1991. "The Geography of the Jews as an Element in Jewish Social History: New York, 1900–1981 and the United States, 1880–1980." Paper given at the Faculty Seminar Israel and Jewish Studies, Columbia University, July 1991.

Rodman, H. 1972. "Marital Power and the Theory of Resources in Cultural Context." *Journal of Comparative Family Studies* 3:50–67.

Rosen, Bernard. 1965. *Adolescence and Religion—The Jewish Teenager in American Society.* Cambridge, Mass.: Shenkman Publishing Co.

Rosenthal, Ted and Barry Zimmerman. 1978. *Social Learning and Cognition.* New York: Academic Press.

Rothman, Jack. 1965. *Minority Group Identification and Intergroup Relations—An Examination of Kurt Lewin's Theory of Jewish Group Identity.* New York: American Jewish Committee.

Rubin, Kenneth, and Hildy Ross. 1982. *Peer Relationships and Social Skills in Childhood.* New York: Springer-Verlag.

Rubin, Lenny. 1995. "Putting the 'Jewish' into Jewish Communal Camping." *Moment* 20, no. 1 (February): 64.

Ruskin, Laurie. 1985. "Adolescent Development and the Jewish Youth Movement," Unpublished. Boston, Mass.

Safilios-Rothschild, C. 1970. "The Study of Family Power Structure: A Review 1960–1970." *Journal of Marriage and the Family* 32:539–552.

Scanzoni, J., and M. Szinovacz. 1980. *Family Decision-Making: A Developmental Sex Role Model.* Beverly Hills, Calif.: Sage Publications.

Scheckner, Jeffrey. 1986. *Issues in Serving Jewish Adolescents—A Background Report.* New York: Council of Jewish Federations.

Schereschewsky, Ben-Zion. 1971. "Adoption." *Encyclopedia Judaica.* Jerusalem: MacMillan Company, Keter Publishing House.

Schiff, Alvin, and Mareleyn Schneider. 1994. *Far Reaching Effects of Extensive Jewish Day School Attendance: The Impact of Jewish Education on Jewish Behavior and Attitudes.* New York: Yeshiva University.

Schwartz, Rachel. 1994. "Going It Alone: Single Parents in a Two-Parent Jewish World," *B'nai B'rith Jewish Monthly,* December, 14–16, 35.

Seader, Mary Beth. 1993. "Adoption: Do Unmarried Fathers Have Rights?" *USA Today,* 26 April.

Seligmann, Jean, and Kendall Hamilton. 1993. "Husbands No, Babies Yes—More Single Women Choose Motherhood," *Newsweek,* 26 July.

Sklare, Marshall. 1982. *Understanding American Jewry.* New Brunswick, N.J.: Transaction Books.

Stonequist, Everett. 1937. *The Marginal Man: A Study in Personality and Culture Conflict.* New York: Russell and Russell.

Strauss, Joan Fuld. 1984. "Child Day Care under Jewish Auspices." New York: Council of Jewish Federations.

Swarttz, Rabbi Michael. 1993. "Camping and Continuity: The Overlooked Connection," *The Broward Jewish World,* 7 October Ft. Lauderdale.

Thomas, John. 1951. "Religious Training in the Roman Catholic Family." *American Journal of Sociology* 57 (September): 178–183.

Tillem, Ivan L. 1987. *The 1987–1988 Jewish Almanac.* New York: Pacific Press.

Strain, Phillip, Thomas Cooke, and Tony Appolloni. 1976. "The Role of Peers in Modifying Classmate Social Behavior." *Journal of Special Education* 10, no. 4 (Winter): 351–356.

Tylor, Edward. 1958. *Religion in Primitive Culture.* New York: Harper and Row.

U.S. Bureau of the Census. 1992. "Resident Population by Age and Race in 1990." *Census of Population and Housing.* vol. 1. Washington, D.C.: U.S. Bureau of the Census.

U.S. Bureau of Labor Statistics. "Statistical Abstract of the United States, 1993." *Bulletin 2340, Table 634.* Washington, D.C. U.S. Bureau of Labor Statistics.

U.S. National Center for Health Statistics. 1994. "Vital Statistics of the United States." *Statistical Abstract of the United States.* Table 142. Washington, D.C.: U.S. National Center for Health Statistics.

Wallis, Claudia. 1987. "The Child Care Dilemma." *Time Magazine,* 22 June 54–60.

Waxman, Chaim. 1983. *America's Jews in Transition.* Philadelphia: Temple University Press.

Weber, Max. 1962. *Basic Concepts in Sociology.* New York: Citadel Press.

Whitehead, Barbara D. 1993. "Dan Quayle Was Right." *Atlantic,* April, 47–52.

Winter, Jerry A. 1989. "Income, Identity and Involvement in the Jewish Community: A Test of an Estimate of the Affordability of Living Jewishly." *Journal of Jewish Communal Service* 66, no. 2 (Winter): 149–156.

———. 1992. "Need for and Use of Jewish Social Service Agencies." *Journal of Jewish Communal Service.* 69, nos. 2,3 (Summer) 75–81.

———. 1993. "Not by Bread Alone: A National Replication and Refinement of a Study of Income, Identity and Household Composition in Jewish Involvements." *Journal of Jewish Communal Service* (Winter/Spring).

Wirth, Louis. 1928. *The Ghetto.* Chicago: University of Chicago Press.

Yaacobi, Gad. 1994. "The Role of Israel in Jewish Education." *Journal of Jewish Education* 61, no. 2: 10–14.

Zahn-Waxler, Carolyn, Ronald Ianotti, and Michael Chapman. 1982. "Peers and Prosocial Development." In *Peer Relationships and Social Skills in Childhood,* edited by Rubin and Ross. New York: Springer Verlag.

ABOUT THE AUTHORS

Ariela Keysar is a Research Fellow at the North American Jewish Data Bank and the Center for Jewish Studies at the Graduate Center of the City University of New York. Dr. Keysar has served as a research associate at the Ratner Center of the Jewish Theological Seminary of America where she coordinated publications of the 1995–1996 North American Study of Conservative Synagogues and their Members. Her Ph.D. in demography is from the Hebrew University of Jerusalem.

Barry A. Kosmin is Director of the Institute for Jewish Policy Research in London, England. Formerly, he was Director of Research at the Council of Jewish Federations and directed the North American Jewish Data Bank. Dr. Kosmin also co-authored a number of books including *One Nation Under God* and *Contemporary Jewish Philanthropy.*

Jeffrey Scheckner is a Research Consultant at United Jewish Communities (formerly the Council of Jewish Federations) and Administrator of the North American Jewish Data Bank. Since 1986, he has co-authored the annual demographic article in the American Jewish Yearbook and has written other publications relating to Jewish social statistics. His M.S.W. is from Yeshiva University's Wurzweiler School of Social Work.

All three authors of this book were also extensively involved in the landmark 1990 National Jewish Population Survey and co-authors of its "Highlights" publications.

Subject Index

Index of Names